The life laundry:
How to stay de-junked forever

Dawna Walter

BBC
BOOKS

To all the contributors and dedicated *Life Laundry* team, who transform chaos into order, even in the most difficult conditions. For my husband, Jerry, who is always my biggest fan, and my mother, Gooch, who is a great inspiration.

This book is published to accompany the television series *The Life Laundry*, produced by Talkback Productions and first broadcast on BBC2 in 2002.
Series editor: Daisy Goodwin
Series producer: Sara Woodford

Published by BBC Books
BBC Worldwide Ltd
Woodlands
80 Wood Lane
London W12 0TT

First published 2003
Copyright © Talkback Productions Limited 2003
The moral right of Dawna Walter to be identified as the author of this work has been asserted.

ISBN 0 563 48749 6

Commissioning Editors: Rachel Copus and Nicky Ross
Project Editor: Julia Zimmermann
Art Director: Sarah Ponder
Design: Grade Design Consultants
Picture Researcher: Miriam Hyman
Production Controller: Belinda Rapley

Set in Helvetica Neue and OCRB
Printed and bound by Bath Press Ltd, Bath
Colour separations by Radstock Reproductions Ltd, Midsomer Norton

BBC Worldwide would like to thank the following for providing photographs and permission to reproduce copyright material. While every effort has been made to trace and acknowledge all copyright holders, we would like to apologize should there have been any errors or omissions.
Abode 57; Alamy 70, 101 right, 105; Andy Stockley 46, 59, 64–5, 71, 77, 118–9, 122–3, 126–7, 130–1; Arcaid 2, 17 left, 40; BBC 6, 17 right, 42, 81, 113; Getty Images 108; Good Homes 9, 12, 16, 43, 49, 54, 60, 66, 68–9, 72, 75–6, 79–80, 85, 93, 97, 101 left; Talkback 52, 114–5; Elizabeth Whiting 14, 18, 21–2, 45, 51, 62–3, 82, 89, 111
Floorplans by Grade Design Consultants and based on original artwork by Andy Stockley at APE Designs.

Contents

Introduction

I am very proud to be a part of the *Life Laundry* programme, most especially because it helps people to take action and move forward in their lives. I often meet people who, through watching the series or reading my first book, *How to de-junk your life*, have been able to take the first step to tackle the clutter in their own lives. Once they began the process of letting go of things that no longer served a useful function or brought them pleasure, they were able to regain valuable space and make the most of their homes. I hope that this second book will encourage those of you who haven't yet taken that first step to do so. For those of you who have already had a major de-junking session, my aim is to help you develop longer-term strategies for keeping your home de-cluttered and loved, ensuring that you are truly making the most of your newly-won space.

When you have made the tough decisions, staying on top of your clutter is a matter of practice. Taking a look on a monthly basis at the habits you have developed can ensure that your possessions never control your life again. By identifying problem areas and taking positive steps to change them, living a cluttered life will remain a thing of the past.

During the filming of the series, we have tackled many areas of clutter that resulted from many different issues, but in all cases our goal was to find the best ways to maximize space and allow people to appreciate their homes and possessions. In each programme we asked our contributors to consider their possessions and let go of those they no longer needed or wanted, to make space for those items they truly appreciated and used. The reward for all their hard work was a redecorated and rearranged space that made it easy for them to find what they wanted and enabled them to appreciate all their treasured possessions.

We all have times in our lives when we find it difficult to stay on top of things. In my life, I find that paperwork can get the better of me and, although I would like to keep on top of it on a daily basis, it often gets put off for more pressing deadlines. The result is that I have to spend a lot more time catching up when I finally get around to doing it – but fortunately I do get around to it on a monthly basis at least. Although I strive for perfection and try to accomplish everything each day, I must often admit my failings and accept my limitations. It never stops me from trying, but makes it a lot less stressful when I don't succeed.

We all need to accept that sometimes it is difficult to manage everything we need to do. Feeling bad about the situation doesn't change things. It just feels bad. Allow yourself some time to relax and plan ways to achieve your goals. As long as you take small steps forward by starting and finishing even an hour's project, you will soon be back on track. If you can find ways of making any process you undertake fun, it won't seem like such a major effort.

In order to become de-junked and stay that way forever, you don't have to live a minimalist existence or control every part of your life. You need to find the level of possessions that makes your house feel like a home that you are fully able to enjoy. To keep your home and possessions looking their best, you have to review your routines and habits on a monthly basis so that you can develop positive practices.

If you have had problems with clutter in the past, making sure you don't repeat the same mistakes takes a constant effort until you no longer find yourself falling back into old patterns. Six weeks of daily effort can help to break ingrained habits and routines. Each day, look at the benefits of living in a home that is clean, organized and ready to enjoy at any time. Walk through each room of your home and survey the situation, noting any areas that require attention. Take positive action to reach the level of tidiness that makes you feel happy in your space.

Once you have pared down your possessions, finding the right way to keep them stored can extend their life and make them easier to use. One of the easiest ways to keep your floors and

surfaces free from clutter is to make sure that everything in your home has a home itself. Finding the right storage solution requires taking stock of what you own. Once you have assessed the quantity of items that need storing, look for areas in your home that could best accommodate them. By using the awkward spaces in understairs cupboards or by chimney breasts, you can maximize your storage.

Every home can benefit from a fresh new look. All too often, once we move into a home and settle in, we rarely go to the trouble of rearranging or updating our furnishings until it is absolutely required. Often, the only time that we think about making changes is when we are ready to leave and sell our home. A fresh coat of paint or revamped space are positive steps that maximize the financial as well as the enjoyment value of your home – why wait until you can no longer reap the benefits of those changes yourself?

In each *Life Laundry* programme, we help to transform wasted space full of beloved but neglected objects into liveable rooms with personal character. To do this, each contributor must confront years' worth of hoarding habits. Often, clutter not only affected their living space, but also their personal relationships. Letting go of the physical clutter often helped to clear the air in these relationships as well. Families working towards a common goal were able to start looking forwards rather than at the past, and let go of the blame. For those living on their own, clearing their space allowed them to feel comfortable in developing new social relationships and allowing people into their homes.

For the entire team, the most joyous part of filming *The Life Laundry* is capturing the expressions of each contributor as they see their reclaimed rooms for the first time. There is always a sigh of relief, not only as the weight of their overwhelming possessions is lifted, but in seeing the magic that the makeover team achieve in such little time. With the emphasis on finding ways to create more space, display treasured items and adapt the room to the needs of each individual, our contributors are able to have the space they always wanted. A few tears are often shed, not the least of them my own, as a fresh path is paved to help them stay on top of their possessions.

Don't let it worry you that you won't have the makeover team on hand to advise – this book is packed with suggestions for helping you to have a go yourself. I too have been inspired by my experiences on *The Life Laundry* to pay more attention to my own home. Although I'm always one for keeping very tidy, not every area of the house was used to its maximum advantage. By reconfiguring two rooms, I have added much more usable space for work and relaxation in my home. Everyone and everything benefits from a bit of attention. Whether it is caring for your personal possessions, or giving a particular room a facelift, a little bit can go a long way in making you feel good about your home.

I want you to think of me as your biggest cheerleader. When confronting your junk, think of me urging you to let go of the things that you no longer use or love. I know that you will be amazed at what a difference it can make in your life.

I start the book with your ultimate goal: how to stay de-junked forever. I ask you to think about the effect that clutter has on your home, your life and relationships. Until you clarify these thoughts, it's difficult to move on. We all take our habits for granted, of course, and it's a great help to step back and actually examine the way we do things. My taking stock survey (pages 22–39) will help you pinpoint problem areas in your life. Once you've analysed these areas, you'll be ready to assess each room in your home to see if you're making the most of every available inch (see pages 41–81). I've included handy checklists to help you focus on essentials and useful hints on storage. Once you've assessed each room, you'll be ready to take on the motivational projects (pages 83–107) that give practical, structured advice on tackling specific areas, from how to organize your wardrobe to making purposeful purchases. Finally, I look at some case histories that illustrate the common pitfalls – how our contributors had become trapped in their own clutter, and how they managed to escape.

I hope you benefit from the many suggested ways throughout the book to help turn your home into the place of your dreams.

Dawna Walter

Staying de-junked forever

De-junking is a way of life, not a one-time experience. Each day you must remind yourself of what you really need and assess whether you are truly using the things around you. Rather than going out and shopping till you drop, getting to grips with what you own and what you use can help you to become aware of your shopping and hoarding habits. Once you see your problem areas, it is easier for you to take steps to stay on top of things. It not only saves you money, but also gives you more space in the process.

In each *Life Laundry* programme, it is easy to see the problem areas of each contributor when their possessions are removed from the rooms we make over. When possible, we gather similar objects together to enable them to see the true patterns of their accumulated possessions. Who can forget the shock when 112 green scarves or 57 red soda siphons were unearthed from hidden-away places? I'm certain that those contributors will be unlikely to make similar purchases in the future! If they begin to lapse into old habits, popping in the video and viewing the contrast of before and after should keep them sorted for life.

If you have had a major purge throughout your home, well done! Taking the first step to get rid of things that you no longer use or like is a massive step forward in leading a de-junked life. Like our contributors, you have become aware of the habits and routines you have developed over years of not getting rid of your stuff. And if you are like our contributors, there is always a lot more stuff that you can sell or give away to free up even more space, as you take control of your possessions.

How does clutter make you feel?

When I visit our contributors for the first time, I am often overwhelmed by the degree of clutter that has accumulated throughout their home. I often feel unable to concentrate as my eye wanders over all the items that have collected over the years. I find it difficult to breathe easily, as often the clutter has been in place for such a long time that layers of dust have accumulated. Just a brief visit can make me feel out of sorts. I can only imagine what it feels like to live with it every day.

When any area of your life or home is filled with clutter, it is difficult to feel at your best. The more things you surround yourself with, either in your thoughts or your material possessions, the more things there are vying for your attention. On a cluttered desk, there are many distractions keeping you from giving your undivided attention to the task at hand. In a cluttered home, it is difficult to feel in control of your possessions. Everywhere you look there is something to do, and if you add to it the responsibilities of bringing up children, it can feel like it is impossible to stay on top of the situation.

The more things around your home that go untended, the more likely you are to suffer from low self-esteem. Everything can become overwhelming, and even the very smallest task can drain you of energy as it seems that nothing you do makes a difference. Sometimes you give up trying until some spark or desire gives you the impetus to make a fresh start.

Left: If your life involves a lot of paperwork, make sure you find a desk to accommodate it all comfortably. Loose papers look untidy and can be misplaced easily.

Clutter can be the basis for anger and frustration, emotions that often make you feel bad on the physical level. When you can't immediately find something you need or trip over piles of possessions that limit your access to areas of your home, you feel the physical results of having too much stuff. Anger, often a contributor to lasting tension, can lead to raised blood pressure and other disorders. Tripping over an obstacle in your path can lead to you seriously injuring yourself. These incidents are a wake-up call to get back on the clutter-free path.

Cluttered areas by their nature are difficult to keep clean. People suffering from asthma or other respiratory ailments may find it more difficult to breathe in a cluttered environment. Anything piled and stacked is a trap for a build-up of dust, leading to a life of grime. The only way to avoid an unhygienic and unpleasant living arrangement is to tackle the tough stuff, one area at a time, and then put in place a regime for staying on top of it for good.

To feel our best we need to achieve balance. Anyone who is on the opposite end of the spectrum and must control everything can have an equally difficult time feeling relaxed and making things happen. Too much time can be spent trying to make things perfect, in a world filled with ups and downs. Balance is achieved when you feel good about yourself and the way you live. Once you have reached the perfect equilibrium, make sure that each thing you bring into your home adds benefit. To keep the status quo, when you bring things in, take other things out.

What do you need to be happy?

As I always say, we are here for a good time, not a long time, so we need to make every minute count. Time spent being unhappy about the circumstances in your life is time you can never regain. Dwelling on the problem areas keeps you stuck there rather than letting go of the worry and taking the action required to change the situation.

One of the many reasons for hoarding things is the fear of not having enough. Some of you may have been influenced by parents or grandparents who experienced rationing during the war and have instilled in you a notion never to throw anything away because it may come in handy. In all likelihood, things accumulate beyond what you will ever use or need, wasting money and taking up space in the process.

For others, material possessions can represent the sense of achievement gained from hard work. Working to be able to provide the luxuries that make life more pleasant is certainly an admirable goal as long as you are doing it for yourself, and not just to impress others. It is also good to have a dream that you can work towards, saving along the way to make it happen.

In the same way that we show off our success from our job-related activities, we sometimes feel like we need physical reminders of our intellectual achievements. Getting rid of books is often a process that can cause emotional distress, as the books represent much of what we have learned over the years. Without the physical manifestation, where is the evidence that we are interesting and intelligent people? In reality, what makes us interesting is where we are now, rather than what we were years ago.

In each room of your home there are essential items that allow you to use the space for what it is intended. A sitting room needs places to sit and a dining room, of course, needs a table. These key items should be the first consideration when looking at the layout of each of your rooms. They should be kept clear of non-essentials to enable you to use them easily and effortlessly at any time.

On top of the essentials, there are the useful items that make life easier and more enjoyable. The only criterion for whether or not

Below: Storage ideas such as these colourful temple baskets are both practical and pleasing to look at. Below right: Books and magazines, if stored properly, can be an attractive feature. Far right: Open-fronted storage helps show off some prized possessions while keeping everything in its place.

they remain in your home is that you use them regularly. We are often inspired to purchase items or gadgets that seem really helpful, and at the time we fully intend to use them. The problem is that usually, after the initial enthusiasm, the thrill wears off and we never actually put them to use. Yet we still find it difficult to throw these gadgets out or to give them away, because we convince ourselves that they will come in handy some day.

To maximize the use of your space and time, each item in your home must be used or appreciated for its decorative or sentimental value. If you haven't used a certain object or looked at it over the last year you should consider whether or not it is something that you really need to keep. In many cases items can be adapted or simply better placed in another area of your home to give them a more useful function.

Often we hold on to items that we don't really use or like out of guilt. Be it an unwanted present from a loved one, or something you purchased and never used, it is better to give it away or sell it to make money for something that would better serve your needs. It is essential to look at the reality of how you use your time and possessions in the present moment to enable you to dig deeper to let things go.

It is, however, the things we cherish that make a house a home. Staying de-junked does not mean that you must live a minimal lifestyle. It means that you use and appreciate everything you own. If your home feels good and brings you pleasure, you have arrived at the perfect balance for you. Don't stop until you get there in each and every room of your home to feel the benefits in how you look, feel and relate to others.

How does clutter affect your relationships?

Whether you live on your own or share a house with others, clutter has a serious impact on social and family relationships. In each home we visit, one of the prime motivators for getting rid of the junk is to allow more social contact within the home and with the outside world. By getting rid of the piles of material possessions that create barriers, it is possible to let go of the past, and start relationships with a clean slate. All the resentments and old habits can be tossed away to enable you to see everyone and everything in a new light.

Sometimes clutter can leave innocent bystanders in its wake. If parents in a household are the most guilty party in allowing possessions to take control, the children always lose out. They either follow in their parents' footsteps, or become painfully aware that the way they live is not the norm, and are uncomfortable inviting friends around. Socializing and play are key factors in developing interaction skills with others, so think about how your clutter can affect your children's development. Is your clutter getting in the way of open communication with your children?

Intimate relationships are also at risk when clutter gets out of control. If one partner is spending more time with their possessions than with the relationship, there will always be emotional upsets. Whether the clutter is work- or leisure-related, it is a way of diverting attention from interacting with each other.

What does the state of your bedroom say about your intimate relationship? By getting rid of the physical barriers, you will create more time and space in which to enjoy being together. At the same time, clearing away the anger, resentment or guilt associated with the clutter opens you to new ways of relating to each other.

We all care, to some degree, about how others view us. Welcoming people into your home allows them to see a deeper, more personal side of your life and encourages more meaningful relationships. When you are comfortable and relaxed in your living environment, your home is most likely also a place where family and friends feel comfortable coming to visit, sometimes at a moment's notice.

When you are concerned about the state of your home, you may not invite people inside. Unable to reciprocate social invitations, you may stop going to visit other people and become more reclusive. If you do let others in, you most probably spend a lot of time apologizing for the way things are. The experience is not a pleasant one for you or your visitors and can leave you feeling isolated and lonely. It's up to you to choose the better option. Do you want a life filled with spontaneity or one in which you feel trapped by your things?

As our contributors clearly prove, the desire to change and some hard work is a sure-fire way to allow more meaningful relationships into your life.

Left: Clothes are often the biggest problem in bedrooms. Wardrobes and chests of drawers should be attractive as well as functional, and provide a surface for displaying favourite photos.

How does clutter affect the value of your property?

If you are a property owner, your house or flat is probably one of your largest assets. In order to see the value of your property appreciate over time, it must be well maintained. The more effort you put into your investment, the greater return you will get, both in financial and enjoyment terns.

One of the biggest problems with accumulating too much stuff is that it gets in the way of seeing the areas of your home that require attention. When your eye is focused on all of the possessions, you don't look at the sagging ceilings, cracks in the wall and unfinished areas that, if left unchecked, can rapidly become major problems.

The more you have, the more there is to clean, and often the task becomes so difficult and time-consuming that it doesn't get done often enough. Aside from the layers of dust and grime that accumulate over time, not looking after your furnishings and possessions properly can also result in an infestation of insects or rodents that can prove difficult to control and can end up lowering the value of your property substantially.

Anyone who has been in the housing market will agree that a tidy and organized space will sell far more quickly and easily than a home that is littered with junk. Buyers can more easily envisage their own belongings fitting into a home if the space is logically laid out with the essentials in each room. The more personal possessions on display that limit the size of the rooms, the less likely you will be able to make a quick sale. Nobody wants to buy a property that appears to have too little storage space to make a comfortable home.

When you look at your property as the sum of all of your material possessions, the way you store them and look after them also has an effect on the value of your property. Throughout our filming we have seen many cases of beautiful furnishings ruined by years of neglect. Whether they are antiques or collectables that may suffer greatly in value by scratches or chips or other damage, or your day-to-day appliances and furnishings whose lifespan is shortened by lack of care, your possessions will never reach their maximum potential value if you do not take proper care of them.

When you care for your possessions, you are looking at and enjoying what you have on a routine basis, which makes it less likely that you will feel the need to buy items superfluous to your needs.

The process of cleaning and repairing items in your home can also help you become more aware of what you actually use and like. Things that have not been looked after for years in all likelihood get very little use or appreciation. More than likely, they have been hiding in a dark corner, obscured by clutter and deteriorating in condition and value.

Assess the value of your home by how well it is maintained. Assess the value of your possessions, by how often you use and care for them. All items that do not add to the value of your lifestyle or home should be given away or sold, to make more space to truly appreciate all that you have and use.

Right: Don't let your most treasured possessions be swallowed up by mounds of clutter. Show them off to their best advantage. A light background helps favourite pieces stand out.

Taking stock survey

We've seen how accumulating too much stuff can have a bad effect on your life and relationships. Your home may not be in as extreme a state as our contributors', but each and every home can benefit from a monthly de-junking routine. One dedicated day each month, or even just a couple of hours here and there, can help you keep pace with the paperwork, manage the wardrobe, top up the staples and enable you to focus your attention on how you are living your life. It can help you to be more productive in both your personal and professional life. Isn't it worth it?

Whether you've already had a major de-junk, are about to undertake one, or need help in just a few areas, these techniques will help you get control of your clutter. Each area of your home should be ready to use for its primary purpose without having to rearrange things. This means that only the essential

items relative to the use of the room should remain there permanently. Simply by taking a look, on a monthly basis, at all the items that tend to accumulate around your home, you can assess your habits and help to keep your space clutter-free 24/7.

The survey is divided up into the areas that I find people often have problems with. You may find that you're coping well in most areas, but just have a weakness for clothes. Or there may be several areas covered by the survey where there is a need for improvement.

In each section of the survey, review your habits over the last 30 days or other suggested period. Note down your scores on page 38 and return to the survey whenever you want to check your progress. Use the helpful storage tips in Chapter 2 (pages 41–81) to find ways of keeping things in their place, or go to the motivational projects section (pages 83–107) for ways to spruce things up in an hour, an afternoon or a weekend.

Left: Make the most of a small walk-in cupboard by using all available wall space, as here by adding built-in shoe cupboards.

Shopping habits

Review your shopping habits to see whether – essential items aside – you purchase items that enhance your life. When answering the following questions, walk through each room in your home and look at the items that you purchased in the last 30 days.

1. How often did you go shopping for non-essential items?

a. daily, or most days

b. weekly

c. when there was something specific you wanted

d. when there was something you needed to replace

2. After you made a purchase, when did you look at it again?

a. sometimes you forgot you bought it

b. when you needed to use it

c. before the end of the day you bought it

d. immediately when you got home

3. Before you made a purchase, did you think about where it would be stored in your home?

a. you bought things you liked and worried where they would go later

b. you bought several things and returned what didn't fit in

c. you took measurements and looked for things that fitted

d. you had a specific picture of what you wanted

4. How often have you used or thought about your recent non-essential purchases?

a. never

b. once or twice to start with, but gradually less

c. routinely

d. all or most of the time

5. How often have you made impulse purchases?

a. daily – whenever you're near a shop

b. weekly

c. once or twice – when you saw something irresistible

d. never

6. How did you feel about the purchases you made?

a. enjoyed it at the time but felt guilty later

b. worried a bit

c. excited about new purchases

d. in control of purchases

Assess your shopping

One of the easiest ways to keep clutter in check is to keep track of new purchases. Each month it is important to look at your shopping habits to see the areas that may need more discipline. It is easy to fall back into old habits if you don't make the conscious effort on a daily basis to plan your shopping times and purchases.

Take a look at how you did over the last 30 days to see if you need to develop better shopping practices. Turn the page to list and assess your purchases.

Shopping notes

Use the space below to record every non-essential purchase you made over the last 30 days. Review your list and use it to pinpoint your weaknesses. Are there any patterns to your buying? If there are three new pairs of shoes on your list, are they sufficiently different to each other, and to what you already had, to justify the expense? Or have you bought three pairs of trainers when you had four pairs already? Put a star next to any items on your list that you can truly say have given you pleasure. Look at any items without a star and try to think about what persuaded you to buy them, and why it is that you don't use them or need them. Jot down your conclusions and list areas that you need to be especially wary of in the future.

_____   _____
_____   _____
_____   _____
_____   _____
_____   _____
_____   _____
_____   _____
_____   _____
_____   _____
_____   _____
_____   _____
_____   _____

_____
_____
_____
_____
_____
_____
_____
_____
_____
_____
_____

Total up your scores by giving yourself
the following points:
A = 10 points, B = 7 points,
C = 4 points, D = 2 points

60–45 points
You may go shopping on a daily basis for
something to do and plan not to buy anything,
but find it difficult to resist. You may come
across something that is inexpensive and
decide to make a purchase, thinking that
because it doesn't cost much, it doesn't really
matter. You have a tendency to leave things in
bags and sometimes may hide them away.
You like to stock up on things so that you
don't run out and, most likely, rarely make a list
of what you are looking for.

See where your weakness lies by
examining your list of purchases. If you shop
at charity shops or go to car boot sales, try to
halve the amount of time you spend doing it in
the next 30 days.
   Go to the motivational projects on pages
83–107 to get some ideas on how to control
what you already own.

44–27 points
You are generally paying attention to your
shopping habits and may go out and splurge
every now and then. You sometimes
purchase more than you intended, and feel a
bit guilty in the process. You like the activity of
shopping but sometimes don't bother to try
things on or make sure that they will be
suitable for what you want, so you end up
returning things.

You could do better in limiting your
shopping. Think about what you want before
you go out shopping and limit your purchases
to those items. Get in the practice of making a
shopping list. Learn the tricks of purposeful
shopping on pages 100–103.

26–17 points
You have achieved a balanced attitude
towards your shopping. You know what you
want and feel good about the purchases you
make. You are likely to use the things you
purchase and enjoy them.

Make the most of them by storing them
properly. Check out the storage tips in the
room-by-room guide (pages 41–81) for easy
and practical ways to keep them at their best.

16 points and less
You are very disciplined in your approach to
shopping and never let it get out of hand. In
most cases you buy things only when
required, and you may not find the shopping
experience a pleasant one. You may have a
tendency to hold on to things until you have
got every bit of use from them.

Lighten up a bit. While it is a very good thing
to use the things you own, it is also good to let
new things into your life every now and then.
Rather than replacing like with like when you
need to shop, try something new. Allow
yourself a luxury from time to time. Get some
helpful tips in the room-by-room guide on
pages 41–81.

Editing habits

By 'editing', I mean the process of selectively reducing the number of items in your home, until you have a manageable number of best items, rather than a mass of clutter you don't really need. Think about how often you've edited your possessions. To stay in control, it is essential that you get into the practice of letting go of things that no longer serve a useful function or bring you pleasure.

1. **In the last 30 days, how often did you get rid of excess paperwork or newspapers and magazines?**
   a. never
   b. looked at them once or twice and got rid of a few
   c. edited weekly
   d. edited daily

2. **In the last 30 days, how often did you go through your refrigerator and food cupboards to dispose of food that was past its sell-by date?**
   a. never
   b. when things began to go off
   c. when you purchased new groceries
   d. daily

3. **When was the last time you looked at and appreciated the things you collect, or pursued hobbies or projects that you had started?**
   a. not in the last twelve months
   b. once or twice in the last twelve months
   c. in the last thirty days
   d. daily

4. **When was the last time you gave away an item of clothing that no longer fitted you or that you no longer wear?**
   a. can't remember the last time
   b. within the last three months
   c. within the last thirty days
   d. within the last week

5. **When was the last time you gave a book away?**
   a. never
   b. when someone wanted to borrow it
   c. when you knew you would not read it again
   d. you don't keep books

6. **When was the last time you sold, gave away or threw away redundant household objects?**
   a. not in the last year
   b. some time in the last twelve months
   c. in the last thirty days
   d. several times this month

Letting things go

Editing your possessions is a form of letting go. Removing things that do not serve a useful function or bring you pleasure can make you feel better on many levels, and as a bonus can give you more space to enjoy your home. When you are unable to let things go without worrying about the consequences, you are placing too much importance on your possessions. Acknowledging that your tastes change or things no longer interest you is a way of allowing new things into your life.

Total up your scores by giving yourself the following points:
A = 10 points, B = 7 points,
C = 4 points, D = 2 points

60–45 points
It takes a lot to get you to let go of things and your home is most likely filled to capacity. If you live in a large house, you may use entire rooms for storing items you do not use or look at. You tend to feel quite emotional about some of your possessions as they represent achievements or memories of past events, and you may tend to worry a lot about being wasteful. You are not happy with the situation but find it difficult to change.

Divide and conquer. Tackle the least emotional area first and follow the getting back to basics section in each room-by-room guide (page 41–81) to see what is truly essential for each room.

44–27 points
Sometimes laziness gets the better of you, and you only take control when it becomes inconvenient to find what you want or you can't relax comfortably. Every now and then you get the motivation for a good clear-out but allow things to build up again gradually. You sometimes feel guilty about not taking the time to take control of your paperwork, or tidy up your home but not guilty enough to motivate yourself into action.

Get motivated to edit areas of your home with some weekend projects to clear your space (see pages 83–107). Tackle the easiest areas first.

26–17 points
You have developed a routine of looking at the things you own and how you use them. You are confident and know what you like and are easily able to take decisions. You do not worry about not having enough and feel good about giving things away.

Maximize the value of your possessions by showing them off to their best advantage. Use Chapter 2 on making the most of your space (pages 41–81) to find new ways to store and display your prized possessions.

16 points and lower
Your home is probably very organized with everything in its place. You may get uncomfortable when you see things that are not put away by others and get up and do it yourself. You are probably quite a visual person and care very much about the way things look.

Your home is meant to be relaxing. If the slightest thing out of place makes you jump up and sort it, you need to spend more time appreciating your space and less time worrying. Limit your tidying to the end of each activity and enjoy it in the process.

Cleaning habits

Keeping on top of your housekeeping will maximize the value of your home and allow you to feel comfortable in your space. Once you get into the habit of dealing with things on a daily basis, you will never allow junk to rule your life again. Look at your cleaning habits, to find any areas that may require a bit more attention to get your home in tiptop shape.

1. **In the last 30 days, how often did your home feel tidy?**
   a. never
   b. for a few days after you cleaned
   c. most of the time
   d. always

2. **In the last 30 days, how often did you put your personal possessions away after use?**
   a. never
   b. when they built up
   c. daily
   d. when you were finished with them

3. **How often do you throw away/recycle used packaging, bottles, papers or household rubbish?**
   a. when they build up
   b. monthly
   c. weekly
   d. daily

4. **In the last 30 days, how often have you vacuumed and dusted all objects in each room in your home?**
   a. never
   b. once
   c. once a week
   d. daily

5. **How often do you thoroughly clean your kitchen and bathroom, including appliances, fixtures and the insides of cupboards?**
   a. haven't done so since you moved in
   b. every few months
   c. once a month
   d. every week

6. **In the last 30 days, how often have you done the laundry or dry cleaning?**
   a. when you couldn't find anything left to wear
   b. when it started to build up
   c. as often as required
   d. daily

Good housekeeping

No one I know would put housekeeping on the top of their favourite things-to-do list, but it is a necessary task that must be done daily to avoid mess becoming a major source of unpleasantness in your home. Living in unhygienic and untidy conditions can waste lots of time and space and make you feel bad about your home or yourself.

Each month, have a good look at all of the areas of your home to make sure things are sparkling clean. See what areas of your home can use a *Life Laundry* clean-up after the last 30 days.

Total up your scores by giving yourself the following points:
A = 10 points, B = 7 points,
C = 4 points, D = 2 points

60–45 points

Your material possessions may prevent you from gaining access to all areas of your home to clean, so you need to take action to clear up everything from the floor and surfaces. If the condition of your home is unhygienic, perhaps you might need to seek help from your local authority to help you clear away the rubbish.

If you are able to tackle it, start with the room that will have the most impact on the way you are currently leading your life. If you live with others, set aside time where you all pitch in for the common good. If you live alone, ask for help. Once you get there, it is easier to maintain.

44–27 points

You have probably developed bad habits over the years, but always make an effort to stay on top of things. You are probably more likely to do the major things like picking things up and vacuuming, but don't seem to find the time to do the more tedious tasks like dusting objects, defrosting the freezer or cleaning furnishings. Things may tend to build up without your noticing.

Sometimes lax housekeeping is due to lack of time and organization. After a long day at work, it can be difficult to get motivated for a major tidy-up. By putting together a reasonable schedule that you are able to maintain, small things on a daily basis and

major things less frequently, it will never reach epic proportions. Check out the top tidying tricks on pages 92–5 to make cleaning less of a chore.

26–17 points

You stay on top of your cleaning but don't worry about making the occasional mess in your home. You are generally tidy and look after your personal possessions. You probably enjoy spending time in your home.

You have developed a cleaning routine that works for you. Make the most of your cleaning time by continuing the editing process. Check any items that you have not used in the last thirty days and see if there are any you can edit.

16 points and under

You spend lots of time cleaning and moving things around in your home, which is a great source of pride to you. You sometimes find that you burn nervous energy by cleaning an area of your home.

It is great to live in a clean environment but, as with everything **balance is necessary** to enjoy your space in all circumstances.

Room reviews

When you are choosing a restaurant or a place to stay, you often look at how other customers reviewed the service, product or accommodation before you take a decision whether to go there. If you had a choice, are there rooms in your home that you would advise against entering? Rate each room of your house over the last 30 days to see how they score.

1. When you entered your home, how often was the entryway free of clutter?
a. never
b. a few times
c. most of the time
d. always

2. Was your sitting room ready for relaxation or entertaining when you wanted to use it?
a. never
b. a few times
c. most of the time
d. always

3. How often have you been able to use all surfaces of your kitchen to prepare your food?
a. never
b. a few times
c. most of the time
d. always

4. How often have you been able to eat your dinner at your dining table?
a. never
b. a few times
c. most of the time
d. always

5. How often would you say you made your bed and picked up all items from the floor of your bedroom?
a. never
b. once or twice
c. mostly every day
d. daily

6. How often has it been easy to find everything you need in the bathroom?
a. never
b. occasionally
c. most of the time
d. always

Room ratings

To help you keep your things under control, it is necessary for you to step back and observe your routines on a monthly basis. If there are particular areas of your home that tend to become a dumping ground for your personal possessions, you can develop better practices to make sure things are tended to daily.

Look at how the rooms in your home measured up over the last 30 days, and see how you can make the most of the space in each of them.

Total up your scores by giving yourself the following points:
A = 10 points, B = 7 points,
C = 4 points, D = 2 points

60–45 points
You have let things slide and feel that you have lost control of your possessions. You may make an effort to clear your space, but end up moving things around and not getting much done. You find it difficult to relax in your home and, each time you need to do something, you first need to clear away the surfaces before you begin.

Get back to basics and tackle one room at a time. Make it a family weekend if you share your home, or set aside an uninterrupted day to have a good edit and clean of the rooms in your home that will have the greatest impact on your day. The most common trouble spots are the kitchen, sitting room and bedroom. Use the motivational projects on pages 83–107 to help with tidying tricks, and the room guide on pages 41–81 for storage solutions to keep your things organized.

44–27 points
You have trouble keeping some areas of your home tidy and seem to have more of a problem with organizing your time than finding the motivation. You like to have things tidy but often feel that things get out of control. You seem to tidy up different areas constantly but never seem to be able to stay ahead of the game.

Setting specific goals for the amount of time you have to tidy can help you get the task done and see some improvement in your living conditions. It only takes a few minutes to make a bed, or hang up your clothing, and getting into the practice of doing it daily can give you greater control of your time and your possessions. For suggestions of how to use your time for constructive projects, turn to pages 83–107.

26–17 points
You take pride in your home and enjoy spending time there. You have good daily practices that allow you to use each room in your home easily for its intended use and rarely do things get out of control. You may have a few areas that could do with better organization, but in general, you are using your space to its maximum advantage.

Get inspired. Now that you have your home in good working order, are there rooms that could do with a fresh look? Try adding some colour or rearranging some furnishings to give your rooms a boost. Look at the motivational projects on pages 83–107 to get some inspiration.

16 points or lower
You strive for perfection and may be a bit out of sorts when things are not perfect. If you live with others, you might find it frustrating if everyone does not seem to share your views on the home.

Strive for balance. Spend time each day focusing on personal relaxation within your home. Create a personal space that you find totally relaxing and that you have control over to help you realize the maximum enjoyment value from your home.

Home improvements

If you look at your home as an investment, putting some effort every month into increasing its value can pay dividends in the future. It also increases the enjoyment value of your space. Home improvements don't require costly solutions. Look at how much attention and care you have put into your home in the last year when answering these questions, then plan small monthly projects to improve your living area.

1. **How soon after you notice a problem in your home do you take action to resolve it?**
   a. you ignore it
   b. the second time you see it
   c. within the next few days
   d. immediately

2. **How many areas of your home require attention?**
   a. all
   b. most
   c. very few
   d. none

3. **How often do you make decorative changes to your home?**
   a. not since you moved in
   b. when it starts to show signs of wear
   c. when you want a change, whether it needs it or not
   d. whenever you see something new

4. **How often do you think about wanting to make changes to your home?**
   a. never
   b. when things don't work
   c. when you are inspired by magazines or places you visit
   d. daily

5. **Do you find that you have to do things perfectly or not at all?**
   a. never
   b. in some areas
   c. can always find a compromise
   d. always

6. **How do you use your home?**
   a. escape whenever possible
   b. it is a roof over your head
   c. you entertain in your home and enjoy being there
   d. you spend most of your time at home

Assessing your home

As one of your largest assets, the physical condition of your home is critical in determining its value. Once you are able to see areas that need work, you can effectively plan ways to get the work done. By ignoring the situation, the value of your property can decrease.

How much effort have you put into your home in the last year? Starting from now, think about what you can do each month to invest in your space.

Total up your scores by giving yourself the following points:
A = 10 points, B = 7 points,
C = 4 points, D = 2 points

60–45 points

You have many problem areas in your home but rarely make an effort to change things. If you do not own the space you live in, you are treating it more like a hotel than a home. If you own the space, you are having a difficult time keeping up with the responsibilities of home ownership.

There can be many reasons why your living space gets the better of you. If excess clutter gets in the way of your seeing the problems in your home, go through the room-by-room guide (pages 41–81) to help you get back to basics. If finances are an issue, try to plan your projects and work towards that end. When you put your maximum effort into finding ways to solve problems, you can come up with many more solutions than you thought possible.

44–27 points

You mostly manage to stay on top of things and your house is in good condition, but perhaps is looking a bit worn and dated. You sometimes think about changing things around but it never becomes a priority and often doesn't get done. You do things when they require attention but do not often do things just for a change.

The value of your home is not just financial. Your home should bring you pleasure. By giving your home a bit of a cosmetic facelift, you can get new energy into your space. Lighten up dark spaces or add some atmosphere to intimate spaces simply by changing the colours on the wall. Look at some of the ways the *Life Laundry* makeover team enhanced the value of the space in each room by turning to pages 46–7, 52–3, 58–9, 64–5, 70–1, 76–7, and the case studies in Chapter 4.

26–17 points

You are able to maximize the value of your home on many levels. You keep things well maintained and update your home regularly. You enjoy living and entertaining in your home and are comfortable having people around.

How much has your home appreciated as a result of your improvements? Get your property assessed and decide whether you wish to move up the property ladder. You may find you have a knack for improving property and making a good profit. If you don't want to move, keep improving your living space to best reflect your creature comforts.

16 points and lower

Your home is very important to you and you pay a great deal of attention to every detail in your space. You maintain and look after your space well and are constantly inspired to change things around and try new things.

Make sure you find the balance between your relationships and your home. Your home should indeed be a work in progress and continue to reflect your current desires. When it begins to take over every minute of the day, learn to appreciate and be content with your current circumstances and enjoy your home with those around you.

Emotional check-up

Excess clutter can lower your feelings of self-worth, make you angry, and make it difficult to relax and enjoy your home. The ability to let go of things enables you to acknowledge that there are cycles to everything in life. When things outlive their useful function or remind you of unpleasant memories, holding on to those items takes up space and keeps you stuck in the past. How you feel in your home is a good indicator of whether you have struck a balance with your possessions. To see how making some personal space for yourself can make you feel better, take a look at how you felt in your home in the last 30 days.

1. **How often did you spend time on yourself for personal relaxation?**
   a. none
   b. a couple of times a month if you're lucky
   c. several times a week for a couple of hours
   d. every day

2. **When you walk into your home, how do you feel?**
   a. tense
   b. resigned
   c. relaxed
   d. excited

3. **Do areas of your home make you feel uncomfortable?**
   a. always
   b. often
   c. occasionally
   d. never

4. **Do you feel in control of your possessions?**
   a. never
   b. some of the time
   c. most of the time
   d. always

5. **Do you find it difficult to take decisions about what to do in your home?**
   a. always
   b. often
   c. occasionally
   d. never

6. **How often have you had a good night's sleep?**
   a. never
   b. occasionally
   c. most of the time
   d. always

Seeking balance

We all have ups and downs, which is part of being human. When you look at how you felt emotionally over the last 30 days, it is important to see if there were any specific situations created by your home environment that caused your emotional levels to be out of balance. These may be one-off things that can easily be sorted. If there are persistent issues that cause you not to feel at your best in your home, take a look at the areas and seek solutions to change them.

Total up your scores by giving yourself the following points:
A = 10 points, B = 7 points,
C = 4 points, D = 2 points

60–45 points

There may be many areas of your life that seem to be out of control, making It difficult for you to get things done and feel good about yourself. You may be spending more time thinking about things rather than actually making them happen, which does not give you a feeling of control over your life.

Do one thing at a time and give it your undivided attention. Confusion occurs when you think too many things at once. Starting and finishing something can boost your self-esteem and make you feel stronger emotionally. Start with the area that you think you can begin and finish in one go and reward yourself when you finish.

44–27 points

You make an effort to keep things on an even keel but sometimes give up too quickly when areas get out of control. You sometimes lack the conviction to take decisions and can be easily led by other people's opinions, leading to a lack of confidence. You need to spend more personal time on yourself.

Take action. Every positive step that you take to be in charge of your own life will give you a greater level of confidence. When you feel bad, what you are doing or thinking about in the moment is not enhancing your goals and objectives. Look at the present and think more about what you desire for the future to make it happen. Look at the case studies in Chapter 4 to see how our contributors were able to move forward with greater confidence after taking control of their possessions.

26–17 points

You have struck a happy balance between home, work and relaxation. You feel good about the state of your home and comfortable throughout your space. You take responsibility for your actions and do not blame circumstances or people around you for what happens in your life. You are able to let things go and allow yourself to enjoy your space.

Maximize the pleasure you gain from your home by creating feelgood places in each room of your home. Look at areas where you would like a bit more relaxation, and incorporate colour, effective storage solutions or luxuries such as scented candles to help create a more chilled-out atmosphere.

16 points and lower

You keep things around you under control and feel good about yourself and your home. The opinion of others may be overly important to you and a motivating factor for trying to have everything perfect. You may be very sensitive and easily upset when things don't always go according to plan.

Try a bit of spontaneity in your life! Every now and then take a few risks and do something out of the blue. Having control over everything doesn't leave much room for the little surprises that come with trying something new and taking a few risks.

Relationships review

Clutter often has an adverse effect on relationships. When piles of possessions build up around you, it can become difficult to communicate with family members or friends. Feelings of anger or guilt can get in the way of open communication. To help you clear the air and improve your social life, take a look at how the state of your home impacted on your personal relationships over the last 30 days.

1. **How often did clutter cause tension in your family?**
   a. daily
   b. several times a week
   c. once or twice
   d. never

2. **How often did clutter cause tension between you and your spouse/partner?**
   a. daily
   b. several times a week
   c. once or twice
   d. never

3. **Did you feel that other people were responsible for the clutter in your home?**
   a. always
   b. most of the time
   c. occasionally
   d. never

4. **How often did the clutter in your home make you want to stay away?**
   a. daily
   b. often
   c. rarely
   d. never

5. **How often did the state of your home prevent you from inviting people to visit?**
   a. always
   b. most of the time
   c. rarely
   d. never

6. **How often did your clutter limit your social life?**
   a. always
   b. most of the time
   c. rarely
   d. never

How do you relate?

Do you and the members of your household or family have different ideas on what makes up clutter? Being able to communicate with those you love and/or live with is integral to having a good relationship. Whenever one party holds ideas different to the other, you either need to find a common ground, or accept the situation without resentment.

Take a look at the areas that caused tension in your relationships over the last 30 days.

Total up your scores by giving yourself the following points:
A = 10 points, B = 7 points,
C = 4 points, D = 2 points

60–45 points

Your relationships are suffering from the clutter in your home, making it difficult to communicate. If you live with others, either you or another member of your family are mostly responsible for the amount of clutter.
If you live on your own and can't let go of things, either family members or friends show some concern for the state of your accommodation.

Ask for help. Just like the families who contact *The Life Laundry* for help, ask friends or relatives, or members of the household, to work together for a common goal. If every individual starts by dealing with their own things, it will make a great difference towards how you relate together as a family.

44–27 points

You sometimes put the blame on others, and you get angry when you have to do other people's chores. You spend a lot of time resenting the things you have to do around the home and it seems to take you a long time to get them done. You find it difficult to deal with others without getting emotional.

Lead by example. Change the things you can change and accept that other people have different values. If you can't live with their habits, bring things to your standards without placing blame and feeling resentful. It is sometimes very difficult to achieve, but worth the effort every time.

26–17 points

It is human to have occasional moments when different opinions collide and cause tension, and this happens to you occasionally. You communicate well with others and feel comfortable to share with those around you. You feel confident to let people into your life.

Plan a group project. If you live with others, or if you are on your own, plan to entertain. A clutter-free existence gives you the freedom to be spontaneous, keeping the house filled with happy moments.

16 points and less

You are a rare creature who never loses your temper with those around you. You may tend to control things but it does not seem to cause any tension in your relationships. Your home is a relaxing place to be. Well done. You probably live alone! Or perhaps you live with people who have similar attitudes. But remember, your home is a place to live in, not a museum, so make sure you enjoy it.

Appreciate your home by planning a celebration! Look for a good excuse to invite people into your home.

Overview

Use the space below to jot down your scores and identify your problem areas.

Shopping habits _____

Editing habits _____

Cleaning habits _____

Room reviews _____

Home improvements _____

Emotional check-up _____

Relationships review _____

Have another go at the survey, say three months after your first attempt, or whenever you feel that you have had time to introduce new routines and habits to your life. Jot down your new scores and see how the two compare. Congratulate yourself on every area of improvement, but also take a note of areas that still need work. Make it your goal to conquer your remaining problem areas too, and try to think of ways you might achieve this.

Shopping habits _____

Editing habits _____

Cleaning habits _____

Room reviews _____

Home improvements _____

Emotional check-up _____

Relationships review _____

Now total up your scores for every category to give yourself an overall survey score.

420–350 points

Clutter and disorder have taken over your life. You are experiencing difficulties in all, or almost all, of the areas examined in the taking stock survey. You feel out of control of your possessions, and behind on your paperwork and general household maintenance. The disorder in your home makes you embarrassed to invite friends over and, if you live with others, is a frequent cause of tension.

Although you have often thought about it, you have never properly confronted your clutter and de-junked your life, as the task always seemed too huge and you never quite found the motivation. But don't despair. It's never too late and now is the time to identify your weaknesses and find strategies for dealing with them. Take a look at the case studies in Chapter 4 to see whether you have fallen into any of the same traps as our contributors to the series. Then turn to the motivational projects on pages 83–107 for advice on how to tackle some of your problem areas.

349–250 points

While you are doing okay in some of the areas covered by the taking stock survey, you are really struggling in others and have days where everything just gets on top of you and drags you down. If you have attempted to de-junk in the past, you probably managed to do a one-time sort-out but didn't address many of the underlying bad habits that led to your clutter problems in the first place. Without confronting these habits and changing them for good, the clutter will eventually always creep back into your home.

Don't be disheartened by any failed attempts to de-junk in the past. Put them behind you and accept that you will have to make some more fundamental changes to your life and routines. Then turn to the motivational projects on pages 83–107 for practical suggestions on tackling some of the most difficult areas.

249–120 points

You are on the right track to leading a clutter-free existence, but there is definitely room for improvement in certain areas. Make the resolution to stop letting yourself down in those areas and try some of the motivational projects on pages 82–107 to get you in the right frame of mind. Take a closer look at each room in your home and make sure that it is as comfortable, welcoming and suited to your needs as it possibly can be. Consult pages 41–81 to make sure that you really are making the most of your space.

119 points and under

You are leading a clutter-free and well-organized existence in a home where everything has its place. You resist the temptation to add endless possessions to what you already have and your close relationships are in good shape. Well done. Just be careful that you're not forcing yourself to live a minimalist lifestyle. Your home should be welcoming and full of the things you love.

Have a look at pages 41–81 for ideas on how to bring out the best in each room in your home.

2

Making the most of your space

One of the greatest rewards of staying de-cluttered is being able to use each room in your home to its maximum potential. The knock-on effect is that you can easily find the things that you want, when you want them, saving unnecessary time and frustration.

One of the most rewarding parts of the *Life Laundry* series is showing our contributors how they can live comfortably, once the clutter is gone. The very talented *Life Laundry* makeover team uses creative storage solutions and design elements to transform each space into a practical and pleasant place to live in.

Get motivated to get back to the basics in each room of your home and look at your space in a new way. Getting your essential items placed to maximize space and light, and using your personal possessions to create atmosphere, can dramatically change how you feel about each room of your home.

Back to basics

Each *Life Laundry* makeover starts by gaining a general understanding of the needs and wants of our contributors. Understanding how they would like to use their space and the items that are really important to them enables good planning that can help to avoid disappointments. Although we never know how many items will end up back in the house, each room is redesigned around the essential and meaningful items that make the space usable and comfortable to live in.

In order to enable our contributors to get to grips with their possessions, we remove all items that are movable from each room we make over to our clutter-busting location. When possible, we put all like things together. Only by looking at the entire picture can our contributors see the patterns in their hoarding habits. By looking at all they have amassed of each item, they can then sort through them to determine which items they use, which items they love, and which items are surplus to requirements. In most cases, over 40 per cent of the possessions brought out on the lawn are able to be disposed of, creating 40 per cent more room to properly store and look after their truly meaningful and useful items.

A *Life Laundry* makeover always starts with a thorough cleaning of all areas of each room. When clutter gets out of control in your home, it is impossible to access many areas easily. Places that are piled high with junk are often hiding years' worth of accumulated dust and grime. Furniture that never gets moved around is a trap for many lost items, and also a collecting point for layers of dust. Even very dark spaces can gain extra light simply by cleaning the light bulbs, windows and ceilings. Naturally, the cleaning isn't the most fun part of the job, but the dedicated team put on some music and get into the swing of

Left: Even your stairs can offer innovative storage opportunities. Right: Prevent outdoor wear from adding to the clutter indoors by keeping it neatly in the hallway. Attractive storage boxes need not look out of place here either.

it all. Starting with a clean slate helps you to see the potential in any room.

There are many elements that, when combined, can help you to bring out the best in each room of your home. First and foremost is using the layout of your room to its maximum advantage. There is always a trade-off between space and stuff, so the more you are able to contain your possessions to the available storage space, the more usable living space you will have. Keeping as much as you can off the floors and surfaces of furnishings will help to give your room a more open feeling.

Once you determine what possessions you need or want in each room, finding the most efficient way of storing them will help to keep them organized and looked after. By finding a home for everything in your home, you can gain valuable time each day from not having to search around for the items you want.

Using colour throughout your home is another element that can make a dramatic change in how you feel about a room. Colours can enhance your ability to relax or be stimulated and can help to create different atmospheres in each room. A very small room can be painted a light colour to make it seem larger, or a deep rich colour to make it appear cosier and even more intimate, depending upon how you would like to use your space. One may be ideal for a home office, the other for a sitting or reading room. For a minimum of effort, you can transform your space in a few hours and give it a whole new lease of life. Have a look at the experimenting with colour section (pages 96–9) for more handy hints.

Your treasured belongings also have a very important role to play in making you feel comfortable in your space. In each programme, we try to restore sentimental items or practical furnishings that have been damaged by years of neglect. When they're cleaned up and either displayed or used, they make your home more personal. In many cases, existing furniture is given a new look and new use by using paint techniques and updated hardware. Updating and modernizing furniture and furnishings is a cost-efficient way of improving the feeling and use in any room in the house.

In our *Life Laundry* makeovers, we try to provide the dream – within the time and budget constraints of the series. In many cases, our fantastic carpenters and builders design and build customized storage solutions for even the trickiest location, to make every bit of space count. The room-by-room guide highlights some of the ways we found to meet the challenge of integrating possessions into liveable and usable space. Some of the solutions may be ideal in helping with your own storage needs.

Get inspired to design your own storage solutions and plan a strategy to get the work done. It may be something that you have to work towards, but the investment will pay dividends in terms of how you use your space and the enjoyment you get from it. The more you think about it, the more likely you are to get it done. Try the motivational projects (pages 83–107) to begin to change how you live forever.

Right: The cupboards in this room are a design feature, providing strong lines and keeping the room symmetrical. They also offer ample storage for clothes and personal possessions. High-level shelving is great for books or ornaments.

Sitting room

The sitting room is often the most public room of your home and should be a warm and inviting space in which guests as well as yourself can feel comfortable. It is a room that should reflect the identity of those sharing the house. Family photographs or other cherished items are often displayed to great effect.

Depending on the size of your home, the sitting room may also double up as the library, home office area, and entertainment room. The more uses the room has, the easier it is for it to become a dumping ground for books, papers, media, games and ignored personal items that make it difficult to use the room for entertaining. When you no longer feel comfortable inviting others into your home, it's time to clear out the junk once and for all.

Below: Our makeover of a contributor's sitting room took its inspiration from the period settee. Below right: By grouping functional things together, we maximized the space, creating different areas for relaxing, dining and working.

Checklist

Sitting room essentials

- Seating for you and guests
- Table lamps for atmosphere and tasks
- Coffee table or end tables
- Shelving or storage units for media and personal objects
- Window treatments
- Dining room table and chairs (if appropriate)

Useful accessories

- Cushions for comfort and decoration
- Baskets to store papers and magazines
- Cabinets to display and protect breakable objects

- Writing desk to keep personal and household papers
- Fireplace equipment and fuel storage (if appropriate)
- Coasters

The personal touch

- Photographs and artwork
- Collections, memorabilia
- Carpet or rug
- Throws
- Television/stereo/media
- Candles
- Drinks cupboard

Before

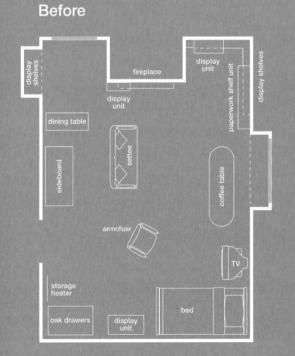

After

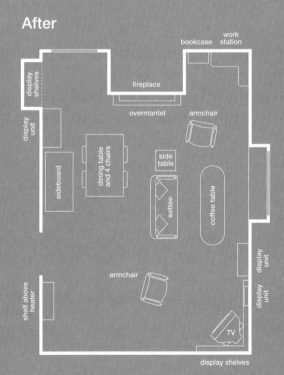

Our sitting room makeovers had a long-lasting impact on our contributors. For the first time in ages they felt proud of their homes and able to relax and entertain comfortably. For one contributor whose sitting room was filled with years' worth of paperwork, excess furnishings and travel gear covering every available surface, we helped to turn his sitting room into a mini Versailles Palace to show off his love of antiques and treasures (see picture on page 46).

The layout

Use the unique characteristics of your space to create the most homely atmosphere. Fireplaces, windows or period details can enhance the look and feel of the space.

In the case of our contributor, the large sitting room was also being used as a bedroom, as there were so many things in the bedroom that he was unable to make room for a bed. By clearing the clutter we were able to give him a proper bedroom with ample clothes storage, and reclaim the sitting room for other purposes.

We took full advantage of the size of the sitting room and created an office and a dining space within it by grouping functional furnishings together. A desk and shelving in a bright corner of the room took up little space

Right: Book cases aren't just for books. Use them to showcase your favourite ornaments, which can add extra interest to a neutral colour scheme.

Storage solutions

Top tips

- Keep your most precious and breakable possessions at higher levels, out of the way of children and pets. Make it a point to dust them on a weekly basis to help them look their best and keep their value.
- We often eat dinner or have drinks in our sitting room space. Fast food containers are big culprits in hiding under furniture. Make it a point to clear all food items each day.
- Don't leave items of clothing to collect in your sitting area. Put things away.
- A rectangular wicker basket is ideally suited to storing newspapers or magazines. Make it a point to get rid of excess papers and magazines daily.

- Utilize unusual spaces. We have created media storage in understairs cupboards and floor-to-ceiling shelving in spaces next to chimney breasts. Maximize your space by going as high as possible.
- Keep control of your books. Often we use our books as a decorative feature in the sitting room. Make sure they are neatly stacked and kept away from sunlight and dust. Leave some spare space for new books to enter your life.
- Keep only the items that you regularly use or truly appreciate in your sitting area. Don't let collections or furnishings get out of hand or the space will feel less relaxing.

and provided ample storage for the office needs of our contributor. A dining room table and chairs fitted neatly against a side wall between built-in shelving units, perfect for storing crockery, glasses and memorable items (see illustrations, page 47).

Think about how you would like to use your sitting room space. Try to create intimate areas for all the activities that you undertake in your room. If reading space is important to you, plan your most comfortable chair to be placed by a window and work from there. Arrange tables or lighting to fit the space.

For many, the sitting room is the main hub of entertainment. Arrange your space so that you are able to accommodate all of your media equipment in that room, bearing in mind that the equipment will need appropriate plugs and sockets. Store your various CDs, DVDs or videos near the relevant equipment. The larger and higher the unit you find to accommodate your items, the more of a design feature it will become in the room.

Back to basics

As the most public space in our home, we often use the sitting room as a showcase for our meaningful items. As in the case of our contributor, his valuable items were precariously placed and not well looked after. Things on display attract dust, so it is important to have easy access to them to keep them in mint condition. Many precious objects can deteriorate as a result of dust and exposure to light or damp.

Look at your key items of furniture and see if there are any that seem out of place. If possible, look for other areas in your house in which they can be utilized. If there are

redundant pieces of furniture, remove them from the space and either sell them or give them away immediately. If they are in bad condition, see if you can get your local authority to come and collect them.

When possible, store like things together. This helps you to see what you own and what you may need to complement your existing possessions. When you have created groups of similar items and know how many of each type you own, look for storage solutions within your home – or in stores and mail order catalogues – to house each group of items. CD racks and bookshelves are good examples of keeping like things together.

Choosing colours

For a harmonious look in a sitting room, choose colours that match one of the key items in the room. In our contributor's sitting room, the design team chose a light blue, to pick up on the colour of the period settee, and all soft furnishings complemented the colour scheme.

If you want the objects in the room to be the centre of attention, a neutral background will show them off to their best advantage. In a museum, the walls are painted white to highlight the art. If you want the room to be more atmospheric, darker and deeper tones such as deep green or dark reds can make the space seem more intimate.

Right: Clever cupboards can make the difference between a chaotic room and a peaceful, stylish one. In this modern room, the wall-cupboard easily accommodates all home entertainment equipment, leaving the seating area clutter-free. Personal items have space to stand out.

Kitchen

There are many ways you can maximize the space in your kitchen without having to go the costly route of a complete renovation. In most cases, a thorough de-junking can help to add at least 30 per cent more working space for food preparation and storage with minimal effort. Using existing storage in an organized way can also help cut down on the time spent in the kitchen.

In many homes, the kitchen is one of the most frequently used rooms and often one of the first stops you make when you get home. As such, it is frequently the dumping ground for post, children's toys and school stuff, pet accessories, clothing and parcels that are brought into the house each day. Unless things are tended to on a daily basis, the mess can quickly get out of control and take over this important family gathering space.

Cluttered kitchens make it difficult to keep up with the essential cleaning that is imperative to limit health risks. Particles of food left in cupboards or on the floor will attract insects and rodents. Overstuffed refrigerators and food storage cupboards mask food kept past its sell-by date – and in the case of one of our contributors, exploded tins of food went unnoticed for months.

Eating and sharing food is one of the most social ways we interact with others. The kitchen, with its wonderful aromas and warm atmosphere, can be the most inviting and comforting room in the house. By efficiently setting up your kitchen space and having a close look at your food shopping habits, you can easily turn your kitchen into one of your favourite rooms in your home.

The layout
If you are not planning a major kitchen overhaul, learn to make the most of your

Right and far right: Keeping surfaces clutter-free is vital for an efficient kitchen. By reorganizing and editing the contents of our contributor's cupboards and giving the open-plan kitchen a new lick of paint, we were able to transform the space without going to the expense of building works.

After

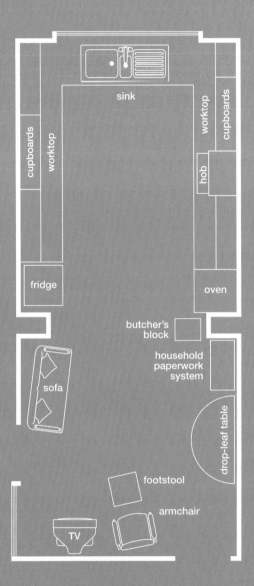

Labels in floor plan:
- sink
- worktop
- cupboards
- cupboards
- worktop
- hob
- fridge
- oven
- butcher's block
- household paperwork system
- drop-leaf table
- sofa
- footstool
- armchair
- TV

Checklist

Kitchen essentials
- Cooker
- Refrigerator
- Sink
- Work surface
- Cupboards or shelving for all storage needs
- Rubbish bin
- Pots and pans that you use frequently
- Cooking utensils
- Cutlery/crockery/glasses (enough for the largest group you entertain)
- Serving bowls
- Spices
- Dried/tinned food
- Water/soft drinks
- Cleaning products
- Cookbooks
- Table and chairs (in shared space)

Useful accessories
- Recycling bin
- Cutlery organizer
- Ceiling rack – if space is limited
- Appliances you use regularly such as: kettle, blender, food processor, coffee maker. Anything you use occasionally should be stored at higher levels in less accessible areas to maximize efficiency of the kitchen,

The personal touch
- Plants/flowers
- Candles
- Photographs/artwork on the walls
- Children's artwork limited to one current project
- Chairs/furniture

existing layout. One of the most valuable assets of any kitchen is the amount of available counter space. In most homes that we visit, clutter has overtaken every free surface, including counter tops, which makes it difficult to prepare a meal easily. Keeping as much stuff as possible off the counter surfaces will make your space look and feel less cluttered.

Where you put your crockery, food and utensils can impact on how easily you use your space. The closer you can store them to where you use them the most, the more time you will save in the kitchen. Pots and pans should be near the cooker, glasses close to the sink, and food that you use most frequently in lower-level cupboards that are easiest to reach. Even these small changes can make your life so much easier.

Below: I like to keep everything out in the open and ready to hand in my colourful kitchen.

If you have a very small kitchen, you will probably need to do your food shopping more often. By keeping your reserves limited to the basics, you will find it easier to keep things contained to the cupboards.

Back to basics

What items do you really use in your kitchen? The primary purpose of the kitchen is to store and prepare food, and in some cases the kitchen is also where you dine. The more activities that take place in the kitchen, the more space is required for proper storage to enable you to keep the counter tops free for food preparation.

Aside from storing and preparing food, the kitchen is often the place where the rubbish and recycling is stored. Finding the proper solutions to contain these functions requires looking for the best use of space. Bins placed inside a cupboard can keep the floors free from excess obstacles that make getting

Storage solutions

Top tips

- Keep like things together. The cutlery drawer is an example of how to store things efficiently in the kitchen. The more you are able to contain like things in the same spot, the less time it will take to find things.
- Take stock of what food you consume on a weekly basis. Prepare a shopping list that takes a complete inventory of everything you use. Each time you shop, top up on essentials to give you one week's worth in reserve.
- Go through your refrigerator and cupboards on a weekly basis to check for out-of-date food. Keep your frozen items only for recommended times.
- Chipped or cracked crockery can be a hazard to your health. Bacteria can lodge between fine cracks and make you ill. Go through all of your cups, glasses and plates routinely and dispose of broken items.

- Keep dried goods in sealed containers. Items such as flour, sugar and rice can easily spill and attract insects. There are many sizes and shapes available in plastic or glass to suit every size of cupboard.
- Never use your oven to store pots and pans. Having to rearrange your kitchen each time you want to cook is demoralizing. Get rid of anything that is non-essential and look at ceiling racks, if appropriate, or metal corner stands that can hold pots and pans.

around your kitchen a strain. Emptying them daily will help to keep your space clean.

As a result of rationing during the Second World War, many of you or your relatives hold on to things that may come in handy. Excess string, bags, or empty jars are often found clogging up the functions of the kitchen. In some cases, even food can be the object of the hoarding. Look at your consumption of the items that get out of control in your kitchen over the next seven days to see how many excess items you have stored. Keep a few weeks' supply and get rid of the rest to help create more space.

If you are like most people, over the years you have collected pots, pans, crockery, glasses, cookbooks and many kitchen gadgets that never get used but continue to take up valuable space. One of the biggest obstacles that gets in the way of having a good clearout is knowing what to do with the excess and redundant items. All too often, rather than going to charity, a car boot sale or even the tip, they end up boxed away and put in the loft or garage. I think there is something in the British psyche that prevents people giving away anything that still has life in it!

Choosing colours

In most homes, the kitchen is the one room where the family are all gathered together at the same time. Kitchen colours should reflect the sociable nature of the area.

As one of the first rooms you spend time in each day, the colour of your kitchen should put you in a sunny mood. You can achieve this either by using the colour itself to get you motivated, or by highlighting the objects in the room that inspire you.

If you have a large kitchen space with lots of objects, artwork or utensils, a fresh white will keep the room bright and airy, and will allow the objects of the kitchen prominence in the space. Deeper colours will make a space seem more cosy and intimate.

When choosing colours for your kitchen, start by looking at the level of light in the room. If your kitchen is dark, keep the walls a light or neutral colour, but add colour to small sections of the space. Multi-coloured tiles as a splashback can add a bit of interest.

Light and bright kitchens are my favourite as they provide great stimulation for cooking and conversation. My own kitchen, pictured on page 54, is one of my favourite rooms in my house, and is painted bright red and orange. The storage cupboards are hot pink and the window treatments combine all three. Every night passers-by have a look inside, drawn to the intensity of the colours. It always breaks the ice when new guests visit.

There are many areas of your kitchen where you can quickly change the look and feel by adding or changing colours. For a quick facelift in our kitchen makeover, we painted the existing fitted cupboards to freshen up the space.

Window treatments such as blinds or curtains can change the atmosphere of the room when light is no longer required. By utilizing colour as an accent to change the mood, you can achieve light, bright and atmospheric effects whenever you want.

Right: A pale colour scheme is the perfect way to brighten up a room that doesn't get a great deal of natural light. Stylish high-level storage cupboards help give this kitchen a contemporary edge as well as keeping work surfaces free of clutter.

Dual purpose or shared bedrooms

The master bedroom is most often the largest bedroom in the house but it doesn't necessarily go to the head of the household. In many cases, it is shared between brothers or sisters in the family if there aren't enough rooms to go around. In one of our stories, brothers aged thirteen and sixteen were required to share a large master bedroom to accommodate their parents' need for home offices. With a complete home reshuffle, the *Life Laundry* team was able to reclaim the master bedroom for the parents and make it work for two uses, freeing up the other rooms for the boys to occupy on their own.

The bedroom is the one room of the house where we must be truly able to relax. In the case of children sharing a space, it is necessary for them to have enough privacy and space to be able to concentrate on their homework or entertain friends to help them develop their interpersonal skills. Sharing with siblings of different ages can make the layout of the space even more important to encourage happy relationships.

In a room shared by adults, the bedroom needs to be an intimate space, and often personal possessions can get in the way. Rooms overfilled with excess clothing, reading materials, business-related materials, children's toys or one person's possessions often create barriers to communication and intimacy, which can all too easily result in frequent arguments.

Right: Think about how you are using every room in your house. In the case of one contributor, the master bedroom worked much better as a double bedroom and home office than as a bedroom shared between two teenage boys.

The layout
The amount of light and the positioning of the furniture can play a key role in how well you are able to sleep or how much you can enjoy your bedroom space to read and relax. All

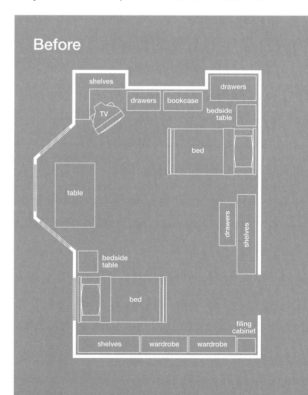

Before

Checklist

Bedroom essentials
- Bed and bedclothes
- Dressing gown, slippers
- Bedside tables or shelving
- Adequate lighting for reading
- Draperies or blinds
- Wardrobe or cupboards for clothing
- Homework, computers, toys/games for children's space

Useful accessories
- Full-length mirror
- Armchair
- Valet-stand to hang next day's clothing
- Laundry basket (if appropriate)
- Wastebin
- Telephone

The personal touch
- Personal ornaments limited to shelving
- Limited books or reading materials
- Artwork or photographs in selected areas
- Rugs or carpets
- Music system, television

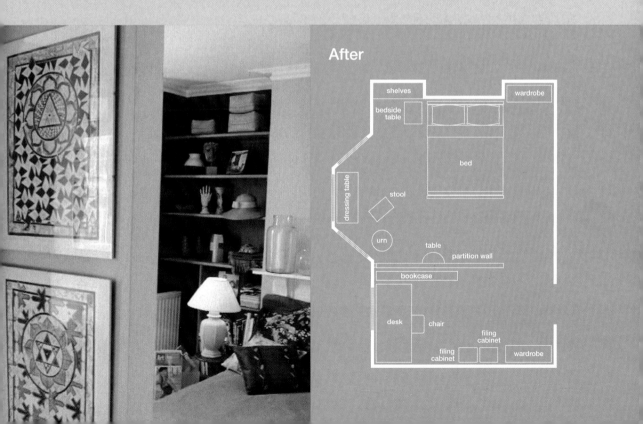

After

shelves · wardrobe · bedside table · bed · dressing table · stool · urn · table · partition wall · bookcase · desk · chair · filing cabinet · filing cabinet · wardrobe

too often, once you move your furnishings into a room, you get used to them as they are and never change things around again to make things work more efficiently. During our *Life Laundry* de-cluttering, all movable items are removed from the space and only those items that serve a useful function or bring pleasure to the contributors are allowed back into the space. To gain a new perspective on how best to divide your large bedroom space into different zones, get back to the very basics. Make sure only the essential items are figured into the equation.

When deciding where to place the key items of furniture, keep clear boundaries between work and relaxation. To create two spaces in one, some sort of divider is the best way to partition off space. In our makeover, pictured on page 59, we built half a partition wall to create a home office within the space of the master bedroom. To divide

Below: This quiet sitting area provides relaxation space in the master bedroom – the perfect retreat if you need time to yourself and the sitting room is too lively.

a large space between siblings, a low-level piece of furniture such as bookshelves can be used as a way of developing borders.

Back to basics

Large rooms often become the repository for many people's personal items, even those who don't share the living space. The larger the space, the more things tend to accumulate rather than being dealt with on an ongoing basis. In our makeover, the boys had not only their own possessions to contend with, but also those of their grandparents who had passed away or who were no longer able to use their things. These items finally needed to be disposed of or found a permanent home, as difficult as this can sometimes be.

Getting rid of all redundant and surplus items is integral to creating a more relaxing environment to refresh your energy during sleep. The most important element is the bed, and it should be placed in an area where you have easy access, if possible from both sides, and have your personal items close to hand.

Storage solutions

Top tips

- When you divide up a larger space, it is to contain activities to a certain area. Whether you create a dressing area, sitting area or workspace alongside your sleeping area, each activity should remain in its own place.
- All surfaces need not be covered with stuff. Keep armchairs free to sit on and desks or tabletops limited to storing those items that you use daily.
- Keep things off the floor. At the end of a long day it is easy to get into the habit of piling things on the floor to be dealt with at a later time. Waking up in the morning to view a chaotic space starts the day on the wrong note.
- Keep the things you use every night close to hand. We all develop bedtime routines of reading, taking off jewellery or instituting a beauty regimen requiring suitable storage. A bedside table or basket near the bed can keep all these items together and out of sight.
- Edit daily the papers that you bring into the bedroom. If you read your post in the bedroom, make sure to take action and file it away in your office work area. Newspapers should be recycled daily and magazines once the new issue is out. Don't let books linger once they have been read.

Most people combine sleeping with dressing and storing clothing so, in order to have a less cluttered space, only the current season's clothing should be stored in your bedroom. Take a look at my tips on how to organize your wardrobe (pages 84–7) for further advice. In excess space, if you are lucky enough to have it, you can create a sitting area to relax or a work area to keep all work-related materials. Don't let them migrate into the sleeping area. The two areas need to be kept separate at all times.

Choosing colours

Colour can be used as a method of visually dividing up space to create different moods or demarcate different activities. The most personal space in the house, your bedroom should make you feel great. If you share the space, make the decision a collective one. Don't be afraid to use different colours in different areas, as long as they all go together to make a harmonious look.

The most important walls of the bedroom are those that you see first thing in the morning as you try to adjust from sleeping to waking. Paler colours or more neutral shades will be the most relaxing and will make the room appear lighter. Brighter shades are more energetic and can stimulate you to get going, but may also keep you awake at night. If you want to use more vibrant shades, the wall where your headboard rests would be the least distracting.

Right: An attic conversion presents a particular layout challenge. Here the workspace is ideally located close to the source of natural light and next to the under-the-eaves storage. The ceiling is high enough elsewhere to accommodate bunkbeds.

Family bathroom

The bathroom is the most personal room in your home and, depending on how many people share this space, may require a variety of storage solutions to accommodate everyone's personal items. Encountering someone else's unmentionables first thing in the morning isn't a pleasant experience.

As a bathroom is a common dumping ground for children's toys, excess laundry, out-of-date cosmetics and endless heaps of towels, it pays to look at your bathroom habits to find the easiest methods to keep the space fresh and tidy. Getting the entire family into the routine of hanging up wet towels and staying on top of the laundry can keep the clutter in check. Having a routine edit of dated cosmetics and bathroom products can clear the decks for a more relaxed space.

Improving the conditions of a shared bathroom can make the beginning of a family day less stressed. Knowing where everything is brings order to the chaos of getting everyone off and ready for the day. Allowing each person who shares the room their own personal space is the ideal way to keep everyone's things in order.

The layout
Often, bathrooms are quite large with lots of wasted space. In both homes that I have

lived in since coming to England, I was able to add built-in wardrobes for my clothing from the under-utilized space. In my case, this required sacrificing a bathtub for a great shower and using the excess space. Any building works can be costly, especially those involving numerous different types. For this reason, before beginning any renovation,

Right: We chose a relaxing shade of pale blue for our contributors' family bathroom and made sure they utilized existing storage solutions, such as this practical cabinet. A high-level shelf for displaying ornaments is an attractive feature.

Checklist

Bathroom essentials
- Fresh towels
- Dressing gowns
- Current bath products
- Current personal hygiene products
- Current grooming items
- Good-sized mirror
- Adequate lighting

Useful accessories
- Towel rail
- Laundry basket
- Medicine chest
- Airing cupboard
- Shelving
- Wastebin

The personal touch
- Plants
- Selection of reading materials
- Area rug
- Ornaments limited to shelving unit
- Scented candles

After

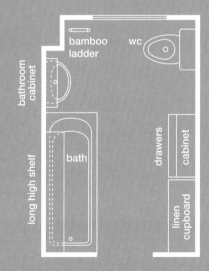

make sure the space you gain is going to be worth the effort.

If you want to make the most of what you already have, assume that the fixtures and fittings will remain in their current location. Because of the time constraints on our makeover team during the filming of *The Life Laundry*, we are able to do only a cosmetic makeover on a family bathroom. But just by getting rid of the junk, changing the colour scheme and using existing storage space more efficiently for housing the daily essentials, the bathroom can become a more harmonious space to start your day.

If your bathroom is on the small side, you will have to work extra hard to find storage solutions and space-saving ideas to store all your necessary items. If you have high ceilings, look for shelving units that utilize the maximum height you have available. Shaker

Below: Try to keep bathtime essentials close to where you will need to use them. A wire rack over the bath is a good solution. If you have a shelf alongside your bath, as here, invest in some storage boxes that blend in with the colour scheme. Wall pegs for hanging up wet towels are also very useful.

peg rails hung at the highest level can make the space look larger by keeping things off the floor area.

Try to look for products that can make awkward spaces work for you. A very practical product is an over-the-loo cupboard, which is available from many mail order suppliers. It is designed to fit around the loo and provides open shelving above it for towels, and doors to keep medicines or personal products hidden from view.

Over-the-door racks can add additional space on the back of a bathroom door. Don't overload them with non-essential items.

Back-up products should be stored in a linen or airing cupboard outside of the bathroom, especially bulky items such as spare loo rolls, towels and cleaning products.

There are many suitable plastic storage options that can usually be stacked or rolled on castors. I always advise clear plastic to allow you instant visual access to what you are storing. Keep like things together and go through each drawer on a monthly basis to keep things current and hygienic.

Keep things to scale. If you have a small bathroom space, try to find the right accessories to fit the space. A laundry basket

Storage solutions

Top tips

- Keep children's bathroom playthings contained in a plastic crate that can fit on the edge of the bath. Limit them to the number of toys that fit in the crate and replace them after each use.
- Colour-code the towels to keep everyone toeing the tidying line. By giving each member of the family a different towel colour, it's easy to spot who isn't keeping the area clutter-free.
- There are many clever bathroom caddies made from either wire or plastic that fit over the head of the shower to keep soaps and shampoo exactly where you need them.
- Shaker peg rails or coat racks are ideal for a heavily trafficked bathroom. Each member of the family can have one hook to hang their towel or dressing gown. You can also give each family

member a kitbag with their personal accessories, helping to keep things off the floor.
- Baskets are a great way to divide and conquer bathroom items. Rolled towels can easily be stored in wicker or rattan baskets, as can spare items too personal to display.
- Do not store unfolded laundry in the bathroom. It can easily get confused with dirty clothing and get washed again and again. If laundry is a big source of bathroom clutter, it must be tended to each day to avoid creating an unsightly and frustrating backlog.

that holds one or two days' clothing is more appropriate than a weekly-sized one. Small spaces require constant upkeep to stay in tip-top form. Empty bottles and excess newspapers or clutter can quickly make the space seem out of control.

Back to basics

Bathing and personal hygiene are the main purposes of this room, so to make the most of your bathroom you need to be able to easily use the space for these functions. Creating storage closest to where you need to use your essentials is most important in the bathroom, as wet surfaces are dangerous. This also requires that you limit the number of personal items that you keep close to hand to only those you use on a daily basis.

Don't be tempted by every new bath product on the market. Limit the number

of products that you buy on impulse by taking stock of what you already have. Allow yourself just one bottle in reserve of any similar product.

The best bathrooms have a good light source, a good mirror and free surfaces to enable you to attend to your grooming needs easily. The closer you can get to the source of natural light, the easier it will be to apply make-up or get a close shave.

Keeping things off the floor is always the biggest challenge, so dedicating as much wall space as possible to shelving and clothing hooks can allow heavy and often wet items a chance to dry and stay fresh for longer. Keeping the floor clear also allows you to get around easily and feel more relaxed as you spend time on yourself.

Choosing colours

When selecting a colour for the bathroom, think about how you use your space. If you need more light to enable you to put on make-up or make the room appear larger, a pale colour is a good choice. Whites and off-whites keep the space looking fresh and clean. Pale shades of blue can be very relaxing.

If you don't use make-up and need a bit more stimulation in the morning, go for a brighter colour. Bright yellow is a good motivating colour. Orange can help to encourage creativity or brighter blues can stimulate your imagination.

Left: If space allows, a wire trolley such as this is ideal for bathroom accessories, products and towels. Right: I divide and conquer my bathroom essentials by putting like things together in colourful baskets.

Children's space

Teaching your children to value their possessions is one of the most important lessons you can pass on to them. To do this, you must lead by example. Until you get to grips with your own possessions, you are paving the way for them to follow in your footsteps. If the general state of the household is chaotic, a weekend spent with everyone tackling their own space can help break old patterns and get everyone set on a new track.

Children physically and emotionally grow up rapidly and can quickly go through clothing, books and toys. If you are planning to increase your family, you may hold on to these items for a future time. Storing them in out-of-the-way locations can help to create more space for your child's development. Encouraging creative play rather than endless

material possessions can help maximize space and enhance children's imagination as well as teaching them good financial lessons.

In all of our *Life Laundry* programmes that featured children and teenagers, it was a joy to see them gladly sell or give away unwanted items. They worked very hard to encourage their parents to let go of as much as possible in order to have a space where they could feel comfortable bringing friends home without embarrassment. The end result was always a more happy and relaxed family.

The layout

The layout of your children's space will change as they develop. At a young age they require more floor area to be able to play safely in their room.

Storage solutions for children's toys and books may need to be at a lower level to

Left: Try to find fun ways of storing toys and keeping them off the floor. Right: A teenager's room is not just used for sleeping in: it must have ample clothes storage and space to work in too. We were able to provide all of this for one contributor in his Eastern-influenced bedroom.

Checklist

Children's space essentials
- Bed
- Drawers for folded clothing
- Wardrobe space for hanging clothing
- Shelving they can reach for books/ toys
- Adequate lighting for each area
- Workspace for homework and creative play
- Wastebin

Useful accessories
- Desktop organizer for pens, paper and creative materials
- Bedside table for personal items
- Under-the-bed storage for larger items
- CD rack or other media storage
- Laundry basket (if appropriate)

The personal touch
- Stereo/television/computer
- Posters or other artwork
- Sentimental objects
- Photographs

After

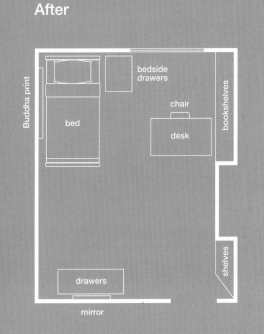

encourage them to put their own things away at the end of each day. There are many accessories available to fit on clothing rails, to allow your children to learn to hang up their clothing. Stacking boxes can grow with them and can be used for clothing or toys. Breakable items will need to be kept at higher levels, out of the reach of very young children.

As they grow older and attend school, the floor area may shrink in order to accommodate larger furniture as well as a desk or work area to encourage good homework habits, creative pursuits and hobbies. At this stage, high-level shelving can be used for books, games, ornaments and clothing.

The older children get, the more surface area and storage solutions they will need for computers, televisions or stereos. Clothing may take up more space as they reach their teenage years, along with additional schoolwork. All of this will create a need for new storage solutions.

Left: By making full use of spaces such as alcoves for shelving, you can free up the remaining walls for other functions – in this case for a climbing wall. To keep the room even tidier, try storing smaller toys and games in labelled boxes that can sit neatly on shelves or under beds.

Back to basics
Because of children's rapid pace of development, it is necessary to have a good edit of their things on a monthly basis. Go

Storage solutions

Top tips
- Keep storage at the right height for children to access to encourage them into the habit of putting their own things away after use.
- Teach them organizational skills by keeping like with like. The more you can simplify where things go, the easier it will be for them to keep things put away. For example, keep all books in one location, all dolls or trucks in another.
- If there's a laundry basket, don't let it become a convenient storage solution. Make sure they hang up things that can be worn again.

- Keep original packaging for games and make sure all small pieces are put away each day.
- A coat rack placed on the wall at the right height can help them organize for the next day. Encourage all school kit to be laid out the night before for a less stressful start in the morning.
- Do a floor check every night, half an hour before bedtime. Make sure that all items are off the floor and in the appropriate place.

through all articles of shoes and clothing for any that have excess wear and tear or no longer fit. Those that can't be immediately passed on to other members of the household need to be disposed of immediately, either sold or given away to charity shops. This will free up a great deal of space instead of allowing out-grown clothes to accumulate to a level where they are out of control. Anything that is damaged, take to the tip. Don't be tempted to hang on to out-grown items of clothing out of nostalgia.

All children's artwork, drawings and homework should be edited down to one or two of the best. To preserve them, invest in a proper portfolio and keep from direct light or damp. All art supplies and homework should be put away on a daily basis to keep the work surface clear for the next day.

All toys should be edited on a monthly basis and new items should be kept in check. Monitor the toys they most frequently play with, to identify which are no longer in favour. When children are very young, you can simply remove the excess items and dispose of them accordingly. As they get older, ask them to decide for themselves which ones can go. Set a number for them to achieve.

As a reward for looking after what they have, children can earn something new. Arrange a pocket money allowance for putting things away each day and helping to keep other areas of the house tidy. It can have a long-lasting effect on how tidy your house will look.

Choosing colours

Using colour to mark different stages of your children's development can help them to feel more grown-up, and more easily able to release the vestiges of childhood. Infants' rooms are most often painted in pastel colours and often have borders or areas of wall treatment. Pale shades of pink, yellow, lavender and blue are all calming. Shapes on wall coverings are often used in early childhood to teach word skills.

As your child gets older, redecorating their room can be a great incentive for them to keep it tidy. As a reward for keeping things in their place over a period of time, let your child choose what colours they would like to have. Each time you update their room, try to get them to dispose of 25 per cent of their things if possible, before starting the redecoration of the room.

Children's rooms have to be multi-functional, serving as a space to sleep and play, and do homework. Select colours based on your children's temperament. If they are very stimulated naturally, choose a lighter-hued relaxing colour such as pink, green, blue, lavender or neutral shades of off-white. If they need a bit more stimulation, try a brighter colour such as yellow or vivid green or blue. You can selectively paint walls of the room where more stimulation is required.

When children reach teenage years, they may desire more atmospheric colours. In our teenage makeover, pictured on page 71, we selected a spiritual, deep green colour to reflect our contributor's passion for eastern culture. Be sure there is adequate lighting and windows if you use darker colours.

Right: Where two children share a bedroom, bunkbeds are the ultimate space-saving idea. Large, heavy-duty trunks make ideal toyboxes and have an old-fashioned appeal.

Home office

Whether you work from home or need to have a place to do your day-to-day household accounts and paperwork, finding a permanent space in your home to do so can be challenging. In many homes, it is not possible to dedicate an entire room to this function, which can often result in paperwork scattered throughout the house. This makes it difficult to find what you need, when you need it, in order to get your projects done. Household paperwork comprises the biggest area of clutter in most homes we visit. Redundant computers and electronics are also big offenders.

When you have to mix living and working space, it is crucial to streamline your paperwork and your storage. In many cases packaging and materials from computers and other electronics take up more space in the room than the work area. It is difficult to concentrate in any area surrounded by clutter as there are too many things vying for your attention and, in a space dedicated to getting things done, you start with a disadvantage.

Throughout the series we have created workspaces in bedrooms, sitting rooms and old storage sheds. In some cases, existing furniture such as a cherished writing desk was restored to its rightful use within a family sitting room. In other cases we custom-built work and storage space in part of a shared-use room that separated work from play. In all cases, adequate storage was provided to keep files current and out of sight.

The layout

In several of our stories, dedicated home office spaces were reclaimed for bedrooms

Left: Box files and stationery holders can create extra storage on top of your desk. Right: If you can't have a separate home office, invest in space-saving and discreet office furniture to create an office in a corner of your sitting room. This was the ideal solution for one of our contributors.

Checklist

Home office essentials
- Desk or other work surface
- Comfortable chair
- Adequate lighting
- Filing system for paperwork
- Place for computers, printers and other equipment
- Adequate electrical and telephone sockets
- Shelving for books and supplies
- Telephone
- In-tray
- Wastebin

Useful accessories
- 30-day accordion file for household bills

- Desktop organizer for pens, pencils and accessories
- Address book including current emergency details
- Notebook to keep track of phone calls or to make lists
- Recycling bin for dated papers
- CD storage
- Clock

The personal touch
- A plant or fresh flowers
- A few framed photographs
- Professional certificates or awards

After

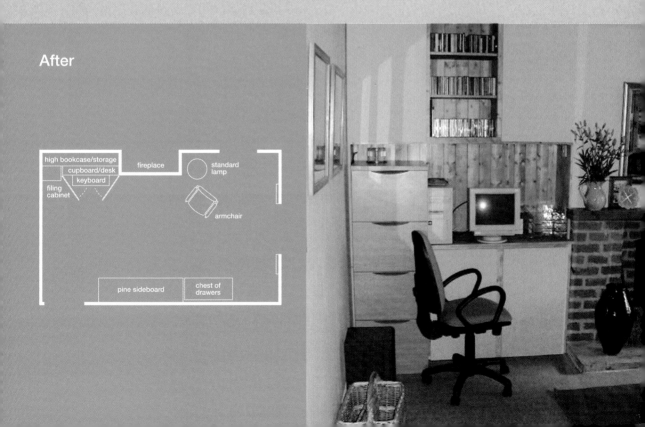

as children got older, and the contents of the home office were integrated into available space in the home. In large spaces, we built a partition wall to separate work and personal space, as we did in a master bedroom and also in a large hallway space. In smaller spaces, we situated the office in a far corner of the room, keeping it isolated from the main activity of the room. Matching the style of the office to the style of the room can also help make it seem to belong in the space.

When looking for the ideal space in your home to situate a home office or personal workspace, find an area in which you are least likely to be disrupted. Placing an office in a heavily trafficked area of your home will make it very difficult to stay focused. Natural light is another important factor in situating a place to work. It helps to keep you awake and is less of a strain on your eyes. You must also think about your electrical and phone line connections when planning your space. Having everything you need to hand will cut down on wasted time.

Back to basics

I will never fully understand all the reasons that we seem to hold on to paperwork, but it is a constant battle to overcome the paper mountain that so easily builds up in

Right: Ample shelving is particularly useful in a home office. Keep key books here and a neat filing system or storage boxes for essential paperwork.

Storage solutions

Top tips

- Get rid of all excess paper as soon as you receive it. Make it a habit to go through bills on a daily basis and get rid of inserts and envelopes that are not needed.
- Move all files that you don't use often to a damp-proof, out-of-the-way location such as a loft or an understairs cupboard. Use sturdy cardboard boxes to file away old tax returns and other documents, making sure to list the contents on the outside of the box.
- Keep as much as possible off your work surface. Papers that are superfluous to what you are working on only cause confusion.

- Metal racks are a good way to access your most often used files. Pick the top five or six projects that you reference most often and place them on a shelf that you can easily reach.
- Edit your files often. Whenever you dispose of appliances or electrical goods, make sure to get rid of warranties and packaging at the same time. When new literature comes in, edit your files of redundant materials.

everyone's home. From personal letters to decades' worth of accounts, often we feel the need to hold on to them as proof those events in our lives really existed!

So what do you really need to keep? Important documents relating to ownership of property, stocks and shares, bank accounts and any other documents that are irreplaceable should be stored in a safe location, preferably with your solicitor. If you choose to store them at home, make sure they are placed in a fireproof metal container. These are readily available in office supply stores. Tax returns and financial information relating to them need to be kept for six years.

You need a work surface – a desk is ideal – and make sure you have a proper chair if you sit down for long periods at a time. A reading lamp is also helpful to keep you from straining your eyes. Bookshelves and a suitable filing system for your paperwork are

also vital to help you keep your items contained in a small area. Everything that is not needed frequently should be stored in out-of-the-way locations such as in the loft or under the stairs.

Choosing colours

Light colours are best suited to office space to help maximize the brightness of the room. Working in a dark, confined space can feel very isolating, especially if you work on your own from home. My home office, pictured on page 81, is in a small half-landing room and has two large windows letting in lots of light. My built-in desk and bookshelf unit are made from birch plywood, a very pale wood that also enhances the light levels in the room. The back wall is painted a pale blue, a colour that promotes calmness, a necessary atmosphere when deadlines loom.

If you require a bit of get up and go to tackle your accounts, try a brighter shade of a light colour. Yellow is a great colour to motivate, and bright green can help you begin new projects. Neutral shades such as off-white or white can maximize light and make the objects in your office stand out more. This can help to keep your mind from wandering.

We have used each of these colours in our office makeovers to fit the needs of our contributors. To select the best colour for your space, take into account the area where your office will be situated. Keeping things harmoniously co-ordinated will help to make your office part of the space.

Left: Storage boxes look tidy, even when stacked on the floor. Right: My custom-built office work surface can fold up to provide more living space.

3

Motivational projects

Take advantage of some of the successful methods we have used to tackle difficult storage and organizational issues by trying our motivational projects to help you on your way to a de-cluttered existence. Our makeover team has only three days to tackle three to four rooms in each house and they always manage to make them look fantastic! It takes dedicated planning and co-ordination but, most of all, having fun in the process and caring about the outcome.

A room makeover should be from the inside out. Contents of drawers, cupboards and other hiding places should be emptied, cleaned and sorted. By looking at your hoarding habits, it is easy to break the cycle of senseless purchases. Re-decorating and shifting things around helps you to learn new patterns of behaviour to stay de-junked forever.

Whether you have an hour, an afternoon or a weekend, choose an area in your home that could use some extra attention and see how good it feels to gain control of your possessions by taking positive steps to make your space work best for your lifestyle. For a complete room transformation, the more time you spend in the planning phase, the smoother the job will go. Make sure to do any bits of shopping required prior to starting the project.

How to organize your wardrobe

Most of us invest a good deal of money in our wardrobe to feel and look our best at all times. The more active the lifestyle we have, the more clothes we collect to meet the demands of home, workplace and recreation.

We are also influenced by the many fashion trends that we see in the media, causing many of us to purchase more and more until our cupboards are bursting at the seams. This results in added wear and tear on your clothing, and a big dent in the chequebook.

Organizing your wardrobe saves you time and money. It enables you to easily find the things you want to wear and allows you to see the many choices you have available. By knowing what you own, you become a better shopper and can still stay current with fashion by updating or accessorizing the things that you already own.

Right: When organizing the clothes in your wardrobe, group like things together.

In under an hour you can get control of your wardrobe rather than letting it control you, simply by putting like things together.

Follow these easy steps to get the job done and gain extra space in the process.

- **Remove all plastic coverings from the dry cleaner's.** They don't allow your clothing to breathe and can fade light and delicate fabrics.
- **Try to avoid using wire hangers,** as they do not lend enough support to your clothing. Suits will stay in shape longer with wooden hangers heavier at the ends to support the shoulders.
- **Hang up all items of clothing in the wardrobe.**
- **Remove anything stored in the bottom of the wardrobe that is not wardrobe-related.**
- **Start with your shortest hanging garments at one end of the cupboard,** ending with the longest garments at the other end, and put like with like – all shirts together, skirts, etc.
- **Colour code clothes in each category:** all white shirts, all beige, all black, etc.
- **Under the short hanging garments you have created extra storage space** ideal for storing shoes, folded clothing or accessories. There are many storage solutions designed specifically to fit in space this size.

So now that you know what you own, do you ever need to shop again? To figure out what you wear, **take the next step.**

Four hours can change your dressing habits forever. Once you have taken the first step of knowing what you own, seeing what you actually wear can be an eye-opening experience – as shared by most of our contributors!

- To start, **set aside four hours of uninterrupted time** and decide that you will get the job done. If you feel like you need a second opinion, ask a close friend or family member whose opinion you absolutely trust.
- **Get enthusiastic** about the project. Anything you can do to make it more fun will make it easier to get through. Uplifting music is a great motivator.
- **Remove any clothing or footwear that is not in season.** These should be stored in less accessible locations such as under the bed, in an understairs cupboard or in the loft – anywhere that they can be away from direct light and damp.
- **Eliminate anything from your wardrobe that you know you haven't worn in the last year, is ripped, permanently stained or doesn't fit.** The reality is that we are human beings and, as such, we occasionally change shape, have spills, buy things we never wear, and often hold on to them out of guilt or for sentimental reasons. Imagine that I am with you, urging you on, and pass them on to a local charity, or make some money at a dress agency or car boot sale.
- **Get out the biggest mirror you own.** One by one, try on each item and see how you look and feel. Put the things that you know you wear back in your wardrobe, making sure to check that they do not need extra care and attention.
- **Look for the similarities in the things you wear.** Are there certain brands that suit you best? Certain colours that you feel good in? Certain styles that fit your body? Make a mental note of the things that work for you.
- **Learn from your mistakes.** Look at the items that you bought and never wear. Think about why you don't like them and the circumstances in which you bought them. Are there any patterns that you can try to change?

To go the distance and turn your dressing area into an oasis of organization and inspiration, **take the next step**.

Over one weekend you can make your dressing area a place that invites you to explore and create new looks. Having all of your clothing and accessories within easy reach reminds you of all the things you have and can inspire you to break the routine of wearing the same things again and again.

Before the *Life Laundry* design team begin any makeover, they have to look at the number of things that need to be stored – down to counting how many pairs of shoes will need to be put away. When they begin, we don't always know what is going back in the house, which makes the job very difficult! Having completed the first two steps, you have already taken the tough decisions, so all you have to do is tally up what you own and look for the best ways to store them.

The *Life Laundry* design team often construct customized storage shelving for use in the wardrobe, but there are so many clever storage solutions on the market that cater to every storage need that you can easily get things off the shelf.

- **The ideal wardrobe is dust-free and out of direct sunlight.** If you store your clothing in anything but a wardrobe with doors, you'll find that dust and light are two enemies of fabric. Add protection and decorative interest to an open-fronted wardrobe with a curtain or cover made from a natural, breathable fabric such as cotton or linen.
- **Put things on display.** Items of clothing and accessories can be beautiful to look at – which is what attracted you to them in the first place! We always display our contributors'

favourite items to make the space more personal. Shoes, handbags, shawls or even neatly stacked jumpers can give your dressing area a personal feel as long as it stays tidy.

- **Dedicate a specific area for each item.** One of the biggest problems in trying to find something is knowing that you keep the same type of things in more than one location. Divide and conquer is a rule I live by and, when planning your perfectly organized wardrobe, look for the storage solutions that can keep all of one thing together. Look for stacking shoe racks, tie racks, belt racks or jewellery organizers that fit into an area where you are most likely to use them.
- **Utilize the space to its maximum advantage.** In older homes there are often awkward spaces that are difficult to find a good use for. Chimney breast alcoves or awkward angles are sometimes difficult to use to their best advantage. Spaces such as these are ideal for built-in shoe and accessory cupboards to utilize the space fully. If you can't spare the expense, take the measurements and adapt a piece of furniture to fit the space.

Getting to grips with home entertainment

The most popular ways of relaxing after a day filled with work or chores are listening to music or watching television or reading. Just how relaxing it turns out to be depends a great deal on how easy it is to find what you are looking for, and being able to sit comfortably in a restful space.

Getting to grips with all of your entertainment media can put you back in control and allow you to access your collections easily, maximizing your enjoyment.

As newer technologies have been developed, letting go of outdated collections that are no longer used can free up space and even generate some income to acquire more current choices.

Right: If you have an extensive CD collection, store those you listen to most regularly on narrow shelves near your music system. Those you listen to less frequently can be kept in clearly labelled CD storage boxes.

UNDER 1 HOUR

In under an hour you can have more relaxing space, simply by having a quick tidy and putting things away.

Follow these simple steps to protect your investment and enhance your time to relax.

- **Put all media back in original packaging.** If some has been lost, most high street music or computer shops sell spares. Make sure to label the contents on the outside of the packaging clearly.
- **Invest in a cleaning kit and dusting cloth for CDs, DVDs and computer games.** Each time you use one, be sure to clean the surface to prevent dust from getting into and building up inside your equipment.
- **Rewind all tapes and videos.** There is nothing more frustrating than having to rewind when you want to unwind! Making the effort to do this when you

put things away will help you make the most of your time.
- **Divide and conquer.** Keep like things together in a storage area close to where they will be used. If you have many of the same items such as remote controls, keeping them contained in a basket will avoid the frustration to trying to find the right one. If they are difficult to distinguish, fix labels to each one.
- **Don't allow papers to pile up.** Relaxation spaces tend to collect other items such as books, papers and magazines. Limit the books to current reading; daily papers should be recycled daily, and weekly publications when the new one is purchased.

You have gained a more relaxed space in under an hour of tidying. To gain more relaxation time, **take the next step.**

Four hours of organizing your media can give you hours of extra relaxation time each week. Once you have taken the first step of putting things away, organizing your media can put you in control of finding whatever takes your fancy in less than a minute. Don't limit your choices to those things you can easily find.

- **Start with the media that you use most often.** Gather your collection from all over your home into one location. The next bit doesn't take your undivided attention, so turn on the music or watch television and have fun in the process. Make piles for each letter of the alphabet and put them in order. Find a storage solution that allows you to keep them all together.
- **Edit media that you no longer use.** Anything that you no longer like should immediately be put aside for selling or giving away. Keep a careful eye on those things that you want to keep but haven't used in a long time. If you don't use them now that you can find them, odds are you never will. Have another edit in three months' time.
- **Check the condition as you sort.** If things no longer work properly, chuck them out. Broken tapes and scratched records and CDs take up space.
- **Put systems in place.** If you often record things from the TV, keeping track of what is on which tape can be a nightmare. Try this efficient system – you will need a notebook and marker. Number your videos on the outside of the box. In the notebook write the numbers of the tapes, leaving several pages for each number. As you record your programme, write it down in the notebook. Cross it out when you record over it and you will have an inventory of all you record.
- **Get rid of redundant media.** Keep on top of the times. If you are holding on to old technology that you never use, get rid of it – it can be difficult to repair and takes up space. Although vinyl and tapes can have a nostalgic appeal, and are sometimes even collectable, for most of us they just gather dust. There are many ways of selling items that are in good condition with original packaging. The Internet provides a great opportunity for sellers and collectors alike. Sites such as www.ebay.com or www.amazon.co.uk provide easy methods of selling online. There are also specialist dealers and auctions for collectable music. Check your local phone book for listings.

To create your ideal space to kick back and relax, **take the next step.**

Over one weekend, you can organize your media throughout your home to create numerous entertainment zones or a personal space just for you. Monitoring your viewing and listening habits can help you to decide on the best places to use and store your gear.

Sound is the most important factor to consider when choosing a space. If you live on your own, it is easy to set up one room to house everything. If you live with others, it can be better to keep each area separate so that everybody can participate in their favourite activity at the same time.

The *Life Laundry* makeover team enabled several contributors to enjoy their passion for music by creating a room dedicated to their listening pleasure. Follow these steps we took to help you get there.

- **Assess the entertainment zones in your home.** If you listen to music or watch television in many areas of your home, each area can be set aside for different parts of your collection, enabling you to easily access the right media where you use it. Dining room music may differ from the music you listen to in the bedroom. Study your habits, and divide your collections up so that you can house them where they are most used.
- **Take stock of what you own.** In the previous steps you organized your media by category and sorted it out alphabetically. Now that you know where you most often use each type, divide them up and count how many go in each area to find the best way to store them.

- **Out of sight, out of mind.** The best storage solutions give you immediate visual access to what you own. Where media plays an important part in the function of the room, wall shelves specific to the size of the media are the best option to keep them in order. There are many inexpensive media-shelving units on the market that can be installed with minimum fuss.
- **Contain your equipment.** Unruly plugs and cables are unpleasant to look at and are easy to trip over. Containing your equipment in one area will keep plugs and cables to a minimum. Get control of your electrics by clearly labelling each connection and wire, making it easy to take apart and put back together.
- **Create the atmosphere.** Entertainment rooms cater to emotions – whether you are cheering on your favourite sports team or getting swept away by a piece of music. Deeper and darker colours are more passionate and can be used to enhance the feelings of the room.

Tidying tricks of the trade

Every home can benefit from a good spring clean – no matter what time of the year! Getting rid of dust and cobwebs and clearing all surfaces of accumulated clutter can immediately make your home feel more spacious. It can also give you the opportunity to see your problem areas, enabling you to put in place new routines to keep things in check.

The more things you have, the more difficult it is to stay on top of the tidying. In many of the homes we visit, piles of possessions limit access to many areas of the home, making it an overwhelming task to tidy and clean.

Once you go the distance and get everything in tip-top order, staying in control of it can be a breeze. By putting in place a daily, weekly and monthly cleaning routine, the job will never get out of hand. Turn up the music, get out the vacuum and duster, and look forward to the end result. It will be worth it.

Right: Once you have proper storage systems in place, staying in control of your things is easy.

UNDER 1 HOUR

In under an hour you can make an impact on any room in your home by removing anything that has collected on the floor or under furniture. A good way to find lost objects and give the carpets a thorough clean, it can also identify bad habits. Learn from your mistakes by paying special attention to problem areas each day.

- **Pick up and put away any articles of clothing.** If you live in a house with many people, each person must be accountable for removing their personal items at the end of each day.
- **Remove any bags or boxes** that may have accumulated in the space. If you haven't looked inside them for the last year, you don't need the contents and they should be immediately disposed of.
- **Don't use the floor as a place to store things.** Find specific storage solutions to contain items that congregate in each room. When possible, keep like with like. Large plastic crates can be appropriate for sporting equipment, while rectangular baskets are great for newspapers, and wall shelving units for media.
- **Fast food packaging accounts for a lot of hidden rubbish.** Very often we put bags and boxes on the floor that can easily get hidden under furniture. Check scary places on a weekly basis to avoid nasty surprises in the future.
- **Keep seating free from clutter.** Remove remote controls, papers, books, craft projects or anything else that can make it a chore to sit down.

Now that you can move around, get down to the nitty gritty and **take the next step.**

4 HOURS

In four hours you can create the illusion of order, just by tackling tabletops and counters. Natural gathering places for all types of items from keys to paperwork, they can easily be a sore spot on the appearance of your space.

Start with the easiest and quickest area to tidy and see what a difference it makes. Go on to the next easiest area and keep going until you have finished an hour's work. You never know, you might get so motivated that you don't want to stop!

- **Papers are the number one culprits.** Get rid of any newspapers older than a day. Junk mail should immediately be recycled. Children's school-related items or household correspondence should be kept in an easy-to-access 30-day file that can be checked and cleared daily.
- **For a thorough clean, remove all items from the surface.** Take this opportunity to see if there are non-essential items that can be moved around or given away. Dust and polish the surface and clean each item. Repeat for all shelves.
- **A place for everything and everything in its place.** We often put things down at the first point we stop at in our home. For many this can be the hallway, or the kitchen. Look at the items that tend to congregate and find the right storage to contain it. Wall-mounted coat racks are a good storage solution for outerwear, keys and pet accessories.
- **Get beneath the surface.** Tackle one specific area and do it thoroughly. If you are cleaning bookshelves or containers that hold objects, take each item out and give the area a thorough clean with appropriate household cleaners. Take the opportunity to edit as you go and next time you won't have to clean so many items.
- **Plants and flowers can be lovely to look at** as long as they are well maintained. They not only need water and light to flourish, but also a proper dusting to enable them to fully breathe. Take this opportunity to dump any that are past their prime and tidy up those that remain.

For the full *Life Laundry* treatment, **take the next step.**

Over one weekend you can thoroughly clean not only what you can see, but also the hidden-away contents of several rooms in your home. Determination and a bit of elbow grease can yield great rewards – more space, less chaos and a more relaxing general atmosphere.

If you live alone, enlist some friends to help out and do the same for them. Anything that you can do to make it more fun will make the chores fly by. If you share a house with others, make it a cleaning jamboree – set aside one weekend when everyone cleans one room from start to finish. Collect all unwanted stuff for charity or a family car boot sale and plan to take it all away by the end of the weekend.

- **Gather your equipment.** Have everything you need to hand to use your time most efficiently. You will need a mop and pail, dusting cloths, sponges, polish, all-surface cleaners, broom, dustpan and vacuum. Make sure you have steps if you need to reach curtains and shelving.
- **A *Life Laundry* clean begins with the ceiling and ends with the floors.** Take down and vacuum or shake out curtains and give fixtures a thorough dusting. Do the same for light bulbs and replace any that may have burned out. A good cleaning session can add a significant amount of light into the room.
- **Wash down the walls.** Outdoor pollution and cigarette smoke along with the daily bumps and knocks can leave stains and dull the walls. If you don't have the time or inclination to

paint, sugar soap is a good way of cleaning up painted surfaces. Follow the cleaning recommendations for different types of paint.

- **Take things out of cupboards.** Out of sight is out of mind and all cupboards are easy places to stuff unwanted and unused items. With minimal effort, you can probably get rid of at least 30 per cent of things that are stored in your cupboards. Take everything out and thoroughly clean the inside before putting back only those items that you use or that bring you pleasure. Place dried cedar or lavender in wardrobes to keep the moths at bay.
- **Hang rugs outdoors for an afternoon to refresh and get rid of excess dust.** Take out your aggressions and beat them with a broom covered in a clean cloth to get rid of maximum dust and debris.
- **Move furniture or appliances away from the wall.** Tackle the out-of-the-way places behind furniture or appliances and give them a proper clean. Wall perimeters are the first place you are likely to spot mice or insects that easily breed among paper and boxes.
- **Rotate cushions and mattresses and give them a good vacuuming.** Food and particles of skin can easily accumulate in places we sit and sleep and are fodder for dust mites.

Experimenting with colour

One of the quickest ways to change the feeling of any space is through the use of colour. From a visual point of view, wall colour can change the size of a room. Lighter colours create an illusion of space, while darker colours make a space feel more intimate or cosy. The size of your room and how much natural light it gets are the first considerations when choosing colours.

White, the absence of colour, can make the objects in a room the focal point of your attention. If you have a lot of artwork on the walls, painting the room a shade of white will least compete with them. Alternatively, you can make particular favourite objects or furnishings stand out in the room by selecting colours that co-ordinate with the most important pieces.

Colour also impacts on how you feel emotionally in a particular space. We all associate colours with different feelings. A blue sky can elevate our mood, while a grey

UNDER 1 HOUR

In under an hour you can narrow down the colour choice, by looking at the light, layout and existing furnishings in your room. With so many paint colours available, you will save time and confusion by knowing what you want.

Follow these easy steps to help you make colour decisions.

- **Look at the size of the room and height of the ceiling.** Decide whether you want the room to appear larger or more intimate. White ceilings will maximize the light in the room. Coloured ceilings will lower light levels and make the room appear smaller.
- **Look at the use of the room.** Places where people gather can support brighter colours, which are more stimulating. More restful places are better suited to lighter and more soothing colours.

- **Look at the time of day you use the room most frequently.** Light levels will change dramatically throughout the day. If you most often use your room in the evening, choose a colour that looks good with limited natural light. If you mostly use the room during the day, you can go brighter as the natural light will make the paint appear lighter.
- **Get some inspiration.** Go through some home interest magazines and see what you like. You can adjust the colour to suit the amount of light and shape of your room. Most paint stockists are now able to mix colours from a photo. Get a sample pot of paint and see how it works for you.

Now that you have developed some ideas, to put them into action, **take the next step**.

and overcast day can have the opposite effect. A bright yellow sun may give us a sense of well being. Red signifies danger, and forces us to stop and look around us. Take a look at the colours that make you feel good and think of ways to incorporate them into your space.

Dare to be different and try something new. If you don't like it, it's only a coat of paint and can easily be changed at not too great a cost. Get thinking about the rooms in your home that might benefit from a new look and feeling, be brave, get inspired and start experimenting.

Below left: Splashbacks and fun accessories, such as this eye-catching mirror, can add extra interest to an already colourful room. Below right: Graphic patterns work well when using bold colours and give the room a contemporary edge. Choose bedlinen using the same palette of shades to keep the look co-ordinated.

In four hours you can completely change the atmosphere of a room by changing the colour on the walls. Colours can stimulate passion, provoke thought, help you to get motivated or make you relax, so use the following guide to choose your colour and paint your way to a better-feeling home.

Red

A very passionate and hot colour, it is not for the weak at heart. It has a dramatic impact on any space and really stands out. It is a very grounding colour and is ideally suited to rooms where people gather, such as sitting or dining rooms. Many shades can also work well in a bedroom.

Orange

Orange is a creative and stimulating colour that works well in kitchens and playrooms. Deeper shades such as terracotta can also work well in a library or sitting room.

Yellow

As energizing as the sun, yellow helps you to get motivated and take action. Wherever a sunny disposition is required, yellow is a good choice.

Green

Green, the colour of nature, is a nurturing colour. Associated with growth, it stimulates you to let go of old ways of thinking. Pale green is good for healing the heart.

Blue

Blue is a very relaxing colour, provided you don't have a tendency to get blue yourself! If you get depressed easily, choose green rather than blue. Many shades of blue are often used in bathrooms and bedrooms. Deep blue is good in rooms where you need to concentrate on something.

Violet

Shades of purple are spiritual colours and are often worn during religious or state ceremonies. Lighter shades are ideal for a bedroom, bathroom or any relaxation room.

Shades of white

White does not provide any energy to the room and makes your possessions appear more prominent. Stark whites are more likely to show off imperfections on walls and can be quite harsh. Off-whites can help the room seem softer.

There are many shades of primary colours to choose from, so look at the feeling you want to create to help you choose the brightness and intensity of the colour. Paint colours look darker on the wall than the paint strips on the tin or colour chart, so try a sample pot before making your final decision.

Don't stop at the walls. To co-ordinate the look and add even more colour to your life, **take the next step**.

Over one weekend, you can complete the re-vamp by changing a few accessories. Once you have changed the colours on the walls, picking up the accent colours throughout the room can help give a more harmonious feel. Often on *The Life Laundry* we find a good scout around the house can yield treasures that match.

If you have chosen a light or neutral colour scheme on the walls, you can accent your room with deeper shades of the same colour. A pale pink room would look good with some red soft furnishings, and a neutral room with deeper shades of brown. You can afford to go bolder with smaller items as they are easy to swap around.

Bright rooms look best with equally bright accessories. If you are going to make a bold statement, carry the theme through. Red walls look best with furnishings of the same intensity throughout. They don't have to be the same shade, but the same intensity works best.

- **Soft furnishings help to complete the look of a room.** Something as small as a cushion can add a colour boost and uplift to a tired-looking chair or add interest to a bed.
- **Window treatments are often the focal point of the room** as our eyes are attracted to the light. If you have special windows and want to make them a feature, use a different colour from that of the walls. If the windows are average, co-ordinate the curtains with the paint colour to make them blend in.
- **Re-discover your treasures.** Part of the fun of changing a room is being able to move things around from other areas of your home. Look for rugs, paintings, pottery or other loose objects that will get a new lease of life in a new home.
- **Flowers or plants are an ideal way to add a splash of colour** and help pull together the atmosphere and look of a room. They can also add fragrance to the room.
- **Grouping like colour ranges together** when placing accessories or objects in a room will give you more impact. A collection of twenty-five white candlesticks would look interesting together, but cluttered if mixed with other things.

How to make purposeful purchases

Knowing what you want when you go shopping can save you time, money and lots of aggravation. Without careful planning, you can miss the integral ingredient for a recipe, or come back with far too many of an item that you already have, creating a need for yet more storage space. Every shopping expedition should have a thought-out purpose in mind.

When you plan your shopping, it makes you keep track of what you have at the moment. If you take a look in your cupboards and check your fridge, you can pretty much sum up what you need. If you make the effort to plan a menu for the week and shop specifically for the relevant ingredients, you will have the satisfaction of knowing that you have what you want for the time being. If you shop at random, odds are you never end up with what you actually need. Even worse, you are likely to end up with plenty of things that you definitely don't need!

UNDER 1 HOUR

In under an hour you can create the perfect grocery list to help you have what you want when you want it. Once you've done it, you can print it off and shave minutes off your weekly shop.

Follow these easy steps to take stock of your cupboards.

- **Divide your list by category** – fruits, vegetables, dairy, meat, etc. – and under each category write down the staple items that you use most frequently in your home.
- **Look at your food preparation over the last two weeks** to find the correct levels of staples to stock. If you use tinned tomatoes several times a week, you want to have just enough to get by with a week in reserve. The items purchased most often will be those with the shortest shelf life, such as dairy and other fresh produce.

- **Think about any items that frequently go off before you use them.** Break the cycle of purchasing those items by finding replacements. Most likely you are shopping out of habit. Maybe it is time to get out the cookbook for new sources of inspiration.
- In your mind's eye, **imagine the grocery store you shop at most frequently.** When you make your final list, divide the categories as they are laid out in your store. If you start at the fruit and vegetable section, place that first on your list and keep as close to the store layout as you can to find everything you need in far less time.

Now that you have sorted your food, to tackle your clothing, **take the next step**.

When you look for something specific, you can limit the confusion caused by having too many things vying for your attention. For example, rather than going in search of a pair of shoes, which could cause you to look in many outlets, thinking about the type of shoes you would like gives them a purpose and function and narrows down your search. You are thinking about what kind of activity you will use them for and which of your clothes they will go well with, rather than being seduced by the moment. By being specific, you can select the best places to find exactly what you are looking for and, with any luck, you'll find just the right thing.

Below left: Unpack your shopping straight away once you're back at home. Admire your purchases for a while if you like, but then store them in their proper place. Below right: For purposeful shopping, make a list of what you need first.

In four hours, you can plan your wardrobe purchases for the season. You start with knowing what you currently own so, if you haven't tackled your wardrobe, follow the under-an-hour quick remedy on page 100. Once everything is divided by category, you can create the perfect wardrobe.

- **Make a list of the different types of clothing you use.** This should include work, special occasion, casual, athletic, outerwear and any seasonal items required. Divide shoes and underclothing into the same categories.
- **Look at how much time you spend on each activity.** If you spend more time doing casual things, you don't need to have so many smart clothes. Your wardrobe should reflect your current lifestyle. Allocate percentages to each of the above categories.
- **Assess your current wardrobe.** Pick out the top 20 per cent that you wear most frequently and examine why they work well for you. See if there are any patterns such as colours you wear most frequently, manufacturers that cater for your body type, or things that you find most comfortable.
- **Look for items that need replacing.** We often wear our favourite clothing over and over again until it wears out. If there are items that have outlived their good looks, pass them on to your local charity shop and purchase a similar replacement. We all have basics such as black trousers or white shirts that are multi-functional and get worn often. The basics never go out of style and are a sound investment.

- **Look for ways to spice up your current wardrobe.** Fashion trends change almost weekly so things that are hot this season may soon date. Check out the current fashion magazines and look at ways of achieving the same style by adding to what you have. High street retailers are always on the ball at interpreting catwalk trends into affordable one-season items.
- **Plan for future events.** If you know that you have some special event you need to attend, don't wait until the last minute to make your purchase. Thinking about the look you want to achieve will help you make a more sensible decision. Determine your budget and set out to find what you want, giving yourself plenty of time.
- **Learn from your mistakes.** If you don't wear something in your wardrobe it is because you don't like it, you don't have a use for it or it doesn't fit. Take this opportunity to let go of anything that is not in use. Look for the patterns in things that are no longer used. Did you buy on impulse? In the sales? Wrong shape? Whatever the reason, banish it from your next shopping list.
- **Plan your expenses.** Once you have made your list, prioritize the things that would be most useful immediately. Look at your budget, think about exactly what you want, and make a list of the shops that will suit your budget. You will find it so much easier to get what you want.

Now that you are fed and clothed, to plan purchases for your home, **take the next step**.

Over one weekend, you can make a plan to have the home of your dreams. Very few people have the financial resources to completely transform their homes in one go. It often takes years of hard work and effort to be able to afford the things we want. Planning what you want gives you a goal to work towards, and can help to focus your purchasing towards these ends.

Start off by deciding whether you really like your home. With all the good intentions in the world, you can't transform something that you intrinsically dislike into something that is your perfect dream. If you see your home as a stepping-stone to help you get to the dream, then your goals should be to plan what improvements would increase the property value to enable you to move on.

During this weekend, make a conscious effort to spend at least an hour in each room of your home. Have a good look around at everything in the room and make a list of things that no longer function or are visibly worn. Does the room provide everything you need to fully appreciate its function? While using the space, think about what things would make it more comfortable or easier to use. Make a list of anything that comes to mind. If you are looking to improve the value, look at adding functional storage solutions that will also let you reap the benefits.

- **Develop a purchasing strategy.** Make a list of immediate, 30-day, six-month and long-term improvements for your home. By directing your attention to the things that you want, it can keep you working towards that goal.
- **Assess the value of your home.** Find out the current market value of your property by looking at how similar properties in your neighbourhood have sold. Many estate agents will give you an estimated value for free. Determine if the cost of your improvements will reap results in the future.
- **Look at the household budget.** Getting to grips with your household expenses can help you to see ways of saving money to achieve your long-term goals. Work out the fixed monthly costs, then look at the capital that you have for future purchases. Try setting aside money each month for a home improvement fund.
- **Do your homework.** The more time and effort you put into the thought process, the more likely you are to make things happen. Research the best products on the market and do some comparative shopping. Waiting until the last minute to make any purchase can be a disadvantage.
- **Get inspired.** Look at home interiors magazines or books and develop your own inspirations file. Keep the interesting bits from the magazines and put them in a ring binder divided by room. Recycle the rest of the magazine to help keep clutter at bay. When the time comes to turn your project into reality, you will have many ideas to get on with.
- **Keep pace with changing attitudes.** Nothing is cast in stone. If your tastes or circumstances change, don't be afraid to change your mind. Goals are fluid, and as your experiences in life change so can your desires. Keep reassessing the goals.

Family clearout

Getting stressed out by other people's mess can put a strain on any relationship. The physical mess is a constant reminder that there is a lack of communication in the household. By developing a happy balance of living standards that each family member agrees upon, you can make your home a much more relaxed environment.

Each member of the household has their own standards of tidiness that have been developed over years of practice. If you are a parent, the standards that you expect from your children, coupled with the example you set, can influence how they live their life in the future. Teaching children to value the possessions they already have is a lifelong lesson that can help to limit the constant desire for new things.

There is no reason why keeping the home ship-shape should be the responsibility of just one family member. If the whole family is involved in keeping the household tidy, then

UNDER 1 HOUR

In under an hour you can set the wheels in motion by organizing a family meeting. Be prepared with a list of improvements that could be make the household run more efficiently. Rather than focusing on all the things that haven't been done in the past and assigning blame, take a positive approach.

- **Walk through the common areas of the house together.** Take note of the trouble spots, without pointing the finger of blame, and look for the best storage solution to solve the problem. Get input from everyone to make sure the solutions will be used.
- **Assign everything in your home its own place, and let everyone know where things are kept.** Be certain that the storage solutions that you put in place are appropriate for the ages of members of your family. Children's coat racks should be at a height they can reach, just as medicine should be at a height they cannot access.
- **Each person should be responsible for putting his or her own things away** as soon as they get home. Personal items belong in your own personal space, and household items should be in the appropriate place.
- **Prepare a list of daily, weekly and monthly chores** and assign different chores to each member of the family. Allow family members to choose their chores, or rotate them, so that different people perform the chores each week.
- **Plan a monthly incentive for working as a team.** We all like a pat on the back, so let each family member pick a treat for the end of the month.

Now that you are all working towards the same goal, **take the next step**.

there is an incentive for each family member to prevent clutter building up in the first place. Your aim should be to get your whole family to recognize the benefits of living in a tidy and comfortable environment, where toys, paperwork and so on can be easily located when needed. Once you all have this mindset, half the battle has been won.

Working together to decide how each member of the family can contribute to keeping the house organized and tidy can help to establish a routine that soon becomes the norm. Once you know what is expected of you, staying on top of the clutter becomes an easier task. In the process, you will gain more time and space and be able to utilize your home to its maximum advantage.

Below: Car boot sales can be a fun family day out and are a great opportunity to get rid of all your unwanted junk. Just make sure you don't come home with even more things!

In four hours you can blitz one clutter hotspot with everyone's help and make your space work better for you. You can all work on one communal space such as the family room, or each family member can tackle their excess books, clothing, media or paperwork and significantly reduce the number of redundant materials that are held on to. By making it a routine practice to stay on top of problem areas, you will be able to see what you own and what you actually use.

Plan one half day on a monthly basis for the family to work together towards reducing the clutter in your home. Start with an area that everyone could bear to reduce and see how much you can let go. Follow these simple steps to help decide what can go.

- **When did you last use it?** Things that have gone unloved and unattended for the last six months are open to negotiation. Anything you haven't used past that time should be immediately passed on to someone who will use it. This can be done through charity, recycling or selling on.
- **Have you looked after it?** You spend a great deal of money on your possessions and, in order for you to gain a maximum return on your investment, they need to be well looked after. Clothing that is routinely left unlaundered will attract months. When it is not properly hung up it will lose shape. Electronic equipment from games to televisions will not last as long as they should if they are not dusted and properly maintained.
- **Do you like it?** Sometimes we misjudge our purchases or get given gifts we don't really like but, rather than be true to our feelings, we hold on to things out of guilt. Honestly assess those items that you have kept out of guilt and finally let them go to make space for new things.
- **Is it in the best location?** Out of sight is out of mind, so make sure that you store your possessions where you are most likely to use them. All too often when things accumulate around the home, you forget what you own. If you haven't missed it, you probably don't need it so be prepared to let it go.
- **Assemble all items that are redundant** to the household and look at the best way to dispose of them.

For a true family affair, make a weekend out of it by **taking the next step** and selling it on.

Over one weekend, you can gather together items in your home that you are ready to sell on, to make a profit at the local car boot sale. In the last two series, our contributors raised from under £100 to several thousand pounds in a programme by letting go of items surplus to requirement, in order to gain space in their homes.

Although many of our contributors enjoyed the experience, in truth it takes the hard work of the entire *Life Laundry* team to pack and set up the pitch. They get up at the crack of dawn for the optimum pitch to maximize the potential reward.

- **Sort through your stuff and know what you have.** Before you go off to the car boot sale, make sure you know the worth of your objects. If you think you have something precious and valuable, seek professional advice from your local auction house. Any information about the history of the object will help professionals to estimate its value.
- **Make the most of what you have.** Clean items using the best methods for the materials. In most cases, the cleaner something looks, the more likely you are to sell it. There may be cases where the age and weathering of an object adds to its value, such as brass, so make sure to read up about anything that may be valuable.
- **Ditch the rubbish.** When going through your stuff for car boot or charity, make sure to first get rid of anything that no one else wants. This includes odd pairs of shoes, soiled or stained clothing or textiles (these items can be re-cycled.) Old tapes, broken or cracked china, opened cosmetics and anything unhygienic. Be sure to use the best methods for disposal.
- **Be prepared.** Bring the necessary equipment to make your stuff look great. Make sure you check out the location and fees and bring along plenty of packing materials. Newspapers and bags are essential. Make sure to have a float and remember to bring enough change.
- **Keep stock.** Label your stuff with realistic prices. Write down anything that gets sold and as the day goes by, lower the prices. Group similar things together and try to stay on top of what you have. The *Life Laundry* team always have a hanging rail for clothing and keep all books or records together.
- **Anything that doesn't get sold at the car boot should be donated to charity.**

The main purpose of the weekend is to see the value of letting things go, both in terms of the space you regain and in terms of the emotional satisfaction and financial reward. Open up your heart, give to others and see what new things enter your life!

4

How it feels to let things go

Once you have made the decision to let things go, there is one word to describe the feeling – FANTASTIC! It seems like the weight of the universe has been lifted from your shoulders and you feel physically and emotionally lighter. In our *Life Laundry* programmes, there is often an emotional release as the effects of losing unwanted clutter allow people to move on into a new phase of their lives. Looking at the rewards of clutter-free living should be a great motivator to help you through the process.

The way you will feel depends on how you look at your possessions. If you hold on to things out of a fear of not having enough, then until you are able to look at what you have rather than the loss, odds are you that you will have a difficult time letting go of things. The only way to rid yourself of these feelings is to actually look at the last time that you used or enjoyed the items, and acknowledge that those that have not been looked at for a long time have outlived their usefulness. Letting them go will give you the freedom to let new things into your life and give you more space to enjoy all that you have.

Moving on

What we own says a lot about our character. Our ability to present ourselves as we choose is fundamental to our individuality. No one has the right to dictate someone's style or say what should or should not be in your home. The key test is how your stuff makes you feel.

My criterion for keeping things remains the same – surround yourself with things that bring you pleasure or serve a useful function. Those items should be appreciated, cherished and well looked after. Everything else is just taking up space. Letting go of the things that are no longer relevant to your current lifestyle allows you to acknowledge who you are in the present moment and to accept that situations in life do change. Allowing yourself to accept those changes opens the door for new and exciting things to enter your life.

Coming to terms with the emotional feelings attached to your possessions can help you to see some of the deeper patterns that cause you to hold on to things. Often, the things you were taught as a child become a part of your adult criteria for what and what not to keep. Those whose parents or grandparents were around during rationing have been taught never to throw things away because they might come in handy some day. Consequently, it becomes difficult to let go of many items in your household that are never used or wanted, but are held on to out of the fear of not having enough.

The ability to forgive yourself and others for things that have happened in your past is another essential factor in moving forward in your life. The reality is that we all make

mistakes – that is what makes us human! Acknowledging and accepting your past mistakes, and letting go of the physical reminders of them, helps to let you see what you no longer want in your life, and allows you to focus on what you do want. Keeping the 'proof' of the mistake just makes you feel bad each and every time you come across it in your home. Stop beating yourself up over things that have happened in the past – it only serves to keep you stuck there rather than looking at all the possibilities the present and future may bring.

Guilt is an emotion that keeps us stuck in the past, and causes us to hold on to things that we don't want, use or enjoy. Often, we are given or inherit items from family members or friends that we feel we must hold on to out of a sense of loyalty to the other person. I have seen many homes filled to the brim with objects that are not really wanted, yet remain taking up space and not allowing the family to express their own identity. Letting go of the objects does not make you forget the loved ones who gave them to you. By keeping those items that you truly love and giving away the rest, you will find a greater sense of well-being which is what those who love you would really want.

In the case of our contributors, their stuff had become a major problem in their lives. In each case, clutter did not allow them free use of their home. In many cases, it created a barrier of communication within households. In some cases, it even created social embarrassment, preventing new relationships from developing. In all cases it had got to the point where the contributors were unable to tackle the clutter on their own.

In the following chapter, we share some of their problems, goals and accomplishments.

Below: When you have whittled your possessions down to the treasured items, even your kitchen shelves can become an attractive display. Try to find a matching set that you really love and that suits your needs. Let unwanted odds and ends go.

How to control the collecting bug

When collections get out of hand, they can begin to consume your life and cause rifts within the family. What was once the pleasurable pursuit of a leisure activity can quickly turn into a consuming force, leaving a trail of neglected objects in its wake. As one of our families came to realize, what may have been planned as an investment for the future did not always result in turning a profit, due to lack of demand or improper care and storage, resulting in damage of the collections.

We start our collecting habits at an early age. From childhood, many of us collect all sorts of things from stuffed animals to toys and games and everything imaginable in between. Many items that we collected during our childhood may continue to interest us into adulthood, or we may find new inspirations to collect. The older we get, the larger the collections grow and often can overcrowd our homes.

Getting to grips with how and why you have become a collector can help you to avoid the pitfall of growing collections without a plan of how to sell or store them. The experiences of our contributors are common to many. Because many items purchased from car boot sales, charity shops or antique shops can be inexpensive, the urge to buy more is ever present. With the best of intentions to sell them on, lack of knowledge or motivation often culminates in accumulating far more than is practical.

Collecting for decoration

Almost all collections start with things that you find interesting to look at, touch or use. Because of the attraction of such objects, they usually begin their life in your home by being displayed or used properly. Pottery and ceramics or old cookware can add great decorative interest to a kitchen. Lace, quilts or photographs are great in the bedroom. Many people collect leatherbound books for the study, or porcelain figures for decorating the sitting room.

Whatever the collection, by grouping it together in a suitable area of your home, you can gain great pleasure from having it on view. Keeping it well dusted and cleaned can help preserve its aesthetic value. Finding the best storage solution to display your collection can also help it maintain its value. Dust, direct light and damp are the three main enemies of many collectable objects.

Although some may find this surprising, I am an avid collector and have many collections displayed throughout my home. I have had a fascination with beads and stones for many years and collect shells and sea glass from various beaches around the world. Some of the most interesting homes that I have visited in many countries have prominently displayed, interesting collections that add charm and character to their space. You don't have to be a minimalist to live a de-junked existence!

Collecting for investment

Like any business proposition, collecting for financial gain requires that it be treated as a proper business. Keeping track of expenses and income as well as having a keen eye, marketing skills, and product knowledge are integral to making it a successful venture.

Before starting a collection to make money, it is important to do your homework. If you find it easy to purchase inexpensive pieces for your collection, odds are that there are many of them in circulation. Unless you are willing to wait for many years to realize a profit, collecting mass-produced items will often not yield great results. Make sure you

Above: Let your collections make an impact by keeping like things together.

don't use the supposed financial rewards as an excuse to increase your collection.

First or limited editions in original packaging and good condition are the safest bet to yield results. Staying focused on one particular type of item rather than a broad range of items will give you a greater sense of market availability and demand. Setting your goals to find the unusual and rare pieces will present a greater challenge and prevent you from purchasing those items that will not add to the value of your collection.

CASE STUDY 1:
FAMILY OR COLLECTIONS:
FINDING THE BALANCE

When one person's collecting habits take up all available space in the household, something has got to give. In the case of our Sheffield family, what started as a weekend activity between husband and wife turned into a major source of resentment in the family.

Our collecting couple began their pursuit before their children were born. They both enjoyed collecting Hornsea Pottery and found that it was readily available from local car boots and junk shops in their area. Each weekend they went out and looked for new items to add to their mutual collection. It seemed an inexpensive way to spend quality time together.

Having grown up close to his uncle who was an inveterate collector, the husband had begun collecting early in his childhood. From military badges and buttons to comic books and records, his fascination with popular culture drove him to begin many collections of objects popular during the fifties and sixties, the period of his adolescence.

Their collecting continued with the birth of their two children and on top of their growing collections came the children's paraphernalia and work-related documents as they both spent part of their time working from home. Before they knew it, their home was so filled with their collections that there was little communal space that reflected traditional family life, causing embarrassment to the teenagers and little space to interact as a family.

Below (left and right): Before and after pictures of our Sheffield family's home office. Once their collections had been edited, they could largely be displayed in the study, leaving the rest of the house clutter-free for the whole family to enjoy.

Before

After

The goals

- Contain collections to specific areas of the house.
- Create personal space in the bedroom.
- Create a family dining space.
- Get rid of duplicates and excess stock.
- Set in place a proper strategy on *buying to sell.*

Solutions

- **Sort out your collections so that you know what you own.** When all of the items were removed to begin our *Life Laundry* de-cluttering, we sorted like with like. Simply by planning to sell all the duplicates, it is easy to reduce most collections by over 40 per cent.
- **Get rid of anything that is broken or in bad condition.** When you don't have proper places to store your objects, things get damaged. In the case of porcelain or ceramics, it reduces their value to almost nothing. It was an eye-opening experience for our contributors to see how many items were cracked or chipped due to mishandling.
- **Learn to discriminate.** Although you may personally find the look of something appealing, it doesn't mean that it is collectable. In the case of this family, with over a hundred soda siphons and few purchasers in the market for them, a space-consuming collection can be relatively worthless. If it is the look you like, limit your purchases to the best representations of the objects that can easily fit in a designated storage unit.

Below (left and right): By removing the clutter and adding a new coat of paint, our contributors' dining room was transformed.

Before

After

- **See what is going on around you.**
When you collect things, you are
sometimes so focused on the object
of your desire that you fail to see what
is going on around you. By always
focusing on your wants, you fail to
appreciate and see all that you have.
In a household, all members need to
have some feeling of connection.
When one person's vision dominates
every area of the home, it reduces the
other members' contributions to family
life, leading to anger and resentment.
- **Be professional.** Selling can be fun
and rewarding as long as you fully
understand everything involved. Start
keeping detailed records of all your
purchases so that you may know how
to price them on for selling. Look at
expenses incurred by renting space at
a fair, advertizing, packaging,
accommodation and travel.

The outcome

After significantly lightening the load of items
to go back into the house, the makeover
team were able to remove all collections from
the master bedroom, creating a neutral
ground for the couple. For the first time there
was wardrobe space to house the couple's
clothing, shoes and laundry. With all
collections removed, there was ample space
to create a relaxed seating and dressing area
to enjoy personal time together.

Most of the collections were housed in
custom-built shelving units in the husband's
home office where they could be fully
appreciated. With everything sorted by
category, it would be easier to develop an
inventory for serious selling.

The dining room contained special
collections that were enjoyed by all. High-
level shelving and a corner cupboard were
ideally suited to showing off the tailored
Hornsea Pottery collection and other special
pieces. The dining room was now a place
that also had family photographs and trophies
to commemorate all who lived in the house.

Living with your inheritance

We sometimes hold on to inherited items out of a sense of obligation. When family members or friends pass away and leave us their legacy, it can feel like a huge responsibility. Not only to we have to cope with the loss of a loved one but, often, we also have to deal with all the things they left behind. Whether you like their possessions or not, it can be difficult to take tough decisions on what items to keep and which to give away or sell. Letting go of the feelings of guilt in making your choices will allow you to appreciate the pleasant memories associated with the most special items that you wish to keep.

Dealing with death is one of the most difficult experiences we have to face. There are many stages to the bereavement process and each individual goes through them in their own time. From the initial shock of hearing the news, to acceptance of what seems like the unacceptable, it can take months or even years to get through. We are often forced to go through our loved ones' homes and personal possessions at the beginning of the process, and taking the first steps to dispose of items can be the most difficult.

Taking the first step

When deciding how best to clear out a loved one's home, it is always easiest to start with the least emotional possessions. If they lived on their own, the general household areas such as bathroom and kitchen can be the best places to start clearing. Be sure to have plenty of support from other family members or friends during the process, and try to concentrate on clearing one area at a time.

This is a time when emotions are at their strongest and, if you are sharing the responsibility with other members of your family, each individual may have their own ideas of what items are important to them. Saying what you want at the outset is the best way of letting others know what is important to you. Many long-lasting family rifts can be avoided during this painful process by having an open dialogue with everyone involved .

One of the nicest ways to pay tribute to your departed loved ones is to let their memory live on through charitable donations. Selecting a charity that will benefit from things that are no use to family members will help you make the initial process of disposing of personal items, such as clothing, an easier task. If you call your local charity and explain the circumstances, it is often easy to arrange a time for them to come and collect things. They may also accept kitchen goods and appliances and household furniture, making it easier to get through the process.

CASE STUDY 2:
THE LAST IN LINE

What happens when you have a distinguished heritage and you are the last in line? For one of our contributors, living with her inheritance meant cramming the contents of a twenty-two-bedroom stately home into a two-bedroom cottage that she shares with her teenaged son. With the addition of left-behind possessions of her two grown daughters, the trappings of a teenage boy and an ever-growing book and CD collection, the tiny, eighteenth-century cottage was overwhelmed with stuff. Not only was their house filled to the brim, but also kind friends and neighbours housed additional furnishings and clothing in their barns and lofts throughout the county.

The great-great-granddaughter of Sir Joseph Paxton, designer of Crystal Palace, she had an interesting upbringing. As the only child on both sides of her family, she lived in a grown-up world. Her father was a journalist who died when she was away at boarding school, in her early teens. Her mother was unwell, and she became the ward of her father's brother, a magazine publisher who also had no children. Her mother died when she was twenty and she inherited all of the family possessions from that side of the family. When her uncle died, she inherited not the stately home – which had previously been sold – but its contents. To settle the estate, many items were brought to auction, and the remaining family treasures were left to her. She felt the responsibility to preserve these items as her children's legacy.

Below: Although our contributor had plenty of beautiful possessions, they were obscured by clutter (left). Just by editing out the superfluous items and introducing some order, the sitting room instantly became more welcoming (right).

Before

After

Rather than taking tough decisions on what should stay and what should be sold or given away, she bagged things up in bin-liners and stored them with friends. On each bag she wrote a date. If it wasn't collected by that date the friends could dispose of it. In this way she gave reponsibility to others for the disposal of her things. Irreplaceable items such as original letters from Sir Joseph Paxton were deteriorating from water damage, and surplus family heirlooms were left untended in the loft. There was no place for guests to stay and beautiful heirlooms were hidden among bags of old clothing, paperwork, hospital equipment from her uncle and stacks of books.

Below: Attic rooms are difficult to get right as the sloping ceiling makes the space an awkward one. Our contributor had originally used hers as a single bedroom (left), but agreed that it worked much better as a study and storage room (right).

The goals
- Preserve irreplaceable items and place them in safe keeping.
- Use the best ways of disposing of unwanted inherited items.
- Create a family sitting room that brings out the best in the heirlooms.
- Create a flexible space that can be used for guests, storage, and a games and computer area.
- De-junk the bedroom of excess books, music and clothing to create a more relaxing space.
- Develop better habits on editing books and paperwork.

Before

After

Solutions

- **Deal with the issues.** An easy solution is to put things in storage and not have to take any final decisions. In many *Life Laundry* programmes and cases that I have seen, fantastic sums of money are wasted by putting things in storage that sit for years unattended. Reducing the number of things you keep can save thousands of pounds.

- **Old letters and photographs easily disintegrate and yellow over time** when exposed to light, air and acids and oil from being handled. To best preserve them, they should be stored in museum-quality acid-free paper and kept away from light and damp. Constant temperatures are best. If they are of particular value, a safety deposit box is highly recommended.

- **You don't have to keep everything you inherit.** In our contributor's case, along with the contents of the house came a hospital bed that she had purchased for her uncle, who used it for only a few days. Not knowing how to dispose of it, she let it sit in the hallway as a catch-all for bags of unwanted stuff. These are the types of items that should be donated to a local charity as soon as possible.

- **Don't let sentiment bog you down.** If there are surplus items that can be sold and the money best put to another use, don't feel guilty. It is more important to be happy living in the present moment, than holding on to things from a sense of duty. In our contributor's case, silver discovered in the loft netted £1,800 from a London silver specialist that could be used for more pressing needs. Bric-a-brac can be taken to a car boot sale or local antique shop along with all pieces of furniture. For better quality items, get several antiques specialists to view them for valuations and choose the best method of selling them on.

- **Once your children have set up their own household, they should take responsibility for looking after their own things.** When their stuff is preventing you from maximizing your enjoyment and use of your space, it's time to get tough. I have many friends who have started their own families and have left stuff with their parents – eventually forcing an ultimatum: take it away or it goes to the tip. Make sure you stand your ground.

- **Avoid the uncertainty.** We often hold on to things because we think our children will want them. Isn't it better to ask their preferences when they reach the right age and know what things they would like to have? As you consider downsizing your space, why not pass things on while you can enjoy them being used?

The outcome

After we left, the family was delighted to be able to have their first guests come to stay in an uncluttered home. Motivated by the experience, they de-cluttered the kitchen, making it much more comfortable and practical to use. And book clutter is a thing of the past after they discovered how to sell old books on the Internet.

Living with children

We all want to do the best for our children, but does this mean that to show them we love them we have to hold on to everything they ever had? How we relate to our children is often a direct result of how we were treated as children. We may share similar tastes, set up our household in a similar fashion, and institute many of the same day-to-day activities as we experienced growing up. In some cases, where childhood experiences were positive, we chose to emulate our parents' lessons. In other cases, where our childhood may hold more challenging memories, we may go to the other extreme to show our children that we love and care for them.

It seems to me that children now have more material things than when I was a child. Whether it is due to more parents both having careers, bringing in more income and sometimes substituting material things for quality time, or simply that children are exposed to more and more things that they want, how your children view possessions will mark their character for the rest of their life. If they are unable to look after them properly, they are not learning the value of their things.

One of the most common problems that we addressed on the *Life Laundry* series was deciding which items of your child's past should be kept. In the most extreme cases, every item of artwork ever done for four children of varying ages kept a family house on the edge of chaos. In another, the parents' lack of organization throughout the house set an example for the children to follow. In both cases the houses were so chaotic that the children felt uncomfortable socializing with friends in their own home.

Leading by example

If you can't bear to part with things, how do you expect your children to do so? Becoming emotionally attached to your possessions makes it difficult to see objectively whether they really serve a useful function or bring you pleasure. Teaching yourself and your children to discriminate and edit constantly can be one of life's most important lessons.

Children are creators from the time they first enter school until the time they finish. They bring home artwork, school exams, projects and trophies that are very important for the moment. Hanging them up is a great way to show them how proud you are of their accomplishments, as long as when new things come home, the old are disposed of.

For sentimental reasons, we often keep the reminders of our children's childhood – first shoes, baby teeth, cards and letters that help to keep these memories preserved for when they are older. But sometimes, in an effort to preserve the past, we fail to see who they are and how they feel in the present.

CASE STUDY 3:
AM I A GOOD MUM?

Our contributors were a family of six, living in a Victorian detached home with a large garden. With four children ranging in age from seven to early teens, the house was bursting with everything the children had ever owned or made, on top of the hoarded collections, work-related items, tools and sentimental items of both parents. Although the house was large and had an addition built a few years before, the more space there was, the more stuff got collected, the end result being spacious rooms that were never used.

For many years of their marriage, the husband worked away from home, often abroad. With four children to look after and serving as both parents, the mum's way of showing love and caring was to keep all of their childhood things. Her own mother

passed away and she had many unresolved personal issues dealing with that time in her life. She treasured all of her mother's items but had avoided going through them until this time.

The husband returned from abroad and began doing some work from home as well as travelling away for several days each week. When he was at home, understandably they chose to go out and do active things together as a family, rather than deal with the backlog of junk that had accumulated. The situation made the mum feel bad about not being able to control the situation, so she decided to call in the *Life Laundry* team to help out.

Below: The rooms in our contributors' house were covered in children's drawings (left). After finding alternative ways to store and display favourite artworks, we were able to de-clutter, re-paint and transform the family sitting room (right).

Before

After

Each room of the house had children's drawings and cards painted years before, and even some of the unfinished walls in the house were written on and painted by the children. None of the rooms could be used to sit comfortably or enjoy family life. The four children shared three bedrooms, but the youngest was determined to have her own space. Refusing to share a room with one of her sisters, she chose to have her wardrobe at the top of the landing, creating a congested and untidy living arrangement. She was also used to sharing her parents' bed – a situation that started at birth and continue. It wasn't a happy situation for any of the family.

Below: Our contributors' large garden room had gradually become a dumping ground for all six family members (left). Once de-junked, the spacious and bright room could be used as a second sitting room and office (right).

The goals

- Return the family room to a more structured area for children to entertain, read and relax. Create storage for books, videos and games.
- Create a room for the youngest child so that she could gain independence from her parents, while keeping her close enough to feel comforted and secure.
- Utilize the garden room for the first time to have a working home office and a place to relax.
- Develop a strategy of learning to let things go.
- Find a permanent home for inherited photographs and letters.

Before

After

Solutions

- **Deal with your own clutter first.**
  Only by coming to terms with the example you set can you expect your children to follow suit. The father was encouraged to go through and edit all of his tools and recreational items to be able to move them into a custom-built home office area in the garden room. This freed up the room attached to the master bedroom for the youngest child.

- **Understand your motivations.** Try not to compensate for what you found lacking in your own childhood by going overboard in the other direction with your children. Very few people have perfect childhoods, so lighten up the pressure on yourself. The mum was able to realize that being a good mum didn't mean that she had to keep everything. Although letting many of their things go was difficult to do, the encouragement of the children to help her through the process made it easier to cope with.

- **Help your children give things away.** Whether the motivation is financial or charitable, teaching children to part with items that they no longer use will significantly reduce the mess in their rooms and make them feel good in the process. Our contributors' children were excited about letting go of old books, clothes, games and especially artwork to make more space to live in. By sending things to local charities, hospitals or playgroups they can see how their cast-offs benefit others.

- **Let your children grow up.** By focusing your attention on how your children are in the present moment, you are more able to deal with the current issues in their life. Holding on and memorializing their childhood memorabilia can often be embarrassing for them. Stick to exhibiting current work and achievements and ask them what things they would like to keep. You would probably be surprised to see how little it is. When all the children of the family got to decide what things they wanted to keep, just a few items were selected.

- **Everyone likes their own personal space.** The move of the youngest child to her own room was a great success. She happily slept in her own bed and loved having all of her things around her. When each child is accountable for the condition of their own space, it is easier to keep things in check. It eliminates the blame culture and teaches responsibility.

The outcome

Once able to see the benefits of a less cluttered space, the family could more easily see the other areas of the house that needed attention. After we left they did a complete overhaul of the kitchen and bathroom, and the next planned projects were to re-do the upstairs bedrooms.

Shop till you drop

There have been many books written on the subject of why we shop, but the *Life Laundry* team looked at the impact that shopping habits can have on how you use your home. When shopping gets so out of control that every inch of your home is littered with material possessions, it limits the possibilities of how you use your space. In extreme cases, it can pose health and safety hazards by blocking easy access to all areas of your home. It also has implications for social and personal relationships.

We all have to shop for the necessities of daily living. With the Internet or mail order, often we don't even have to leave our homes to get what we want delivered directly to our door. It is also one the most common leisure activities. Going out with friends to have a look in the shops is a way of spending an afternoon out and doesn't necessarily require that you purchase anything. Window-shopping can give you the inspiration to use your existing things in a new way.

Excessive shopping can often occur as a result of a change in your daily routine. If you have been employed and suddenly stop working, going out each day can fill a void left by your previous routine and can easily lead to acquiring things out of habit. Often, inexpensive purchases from junk or charity shops seem insignificant at the time, but cumulatively add up to lots of money wasted on items that will never be used. To regain control over your shopping habits, have a look at pages 100–103.

Take stock before you shop

To run a successful business you must retain tight controls of your inventory. Having too many items of the same thing means that customers are not purchasing them. They are taking up space without turning a profit. Those items that are out of stock and in demand are lost sales causing customer dissatisfaction. Both situations limit your cash flow and can end in disaster. Running a household works on the same principle. Too much of the same thing takes up valuable space and wastes your most precious asset. Not having what you need, when you need it, can lead to anger and frustration.

Planning your purchases is the best way to ensure that you don't buy more than you need. By keeping focused on finding exactly what you are looking for, you can take your time with each purchase and visit many shops before making your final decision. This way you can still shop at length, but sensibly.

Finding a home for everything in your house will help you take stock of what you have. Keeping all like things together in one place will help you see the areas that may be getting out of control. When you get to the point where you are hiding things away in bin-liners, it's time to face up to the problem and take control of your possessions.

CASE STUDY 4:
TALES OF A SELF-
CONFESSED SHOPAHOLIC

Sometimes it takes a specific goal to make you want to get your house in order. In the case of our *Life Laundry* contributor, her desire to reciprocate the kindness of free lodging while singing abroad was the motivation it took to get rid of years' worth of over-shopping. Declaring war on the hundreds of bin-liners filled to the brim with charity shop purchases, we set out to find the bed in what was once a guest room to help make that dream come true.

An only child of older parents who long since passed away, she grew up in a religious and very austere home and was often ill as a child. Not allowed to socialize with other children, she spent any available opportunity listening to music, which, too, was often denied her. Whatever caused her

to shop until she could barely enter several of her rooms, she was now ready to clear the physical reminders of her shopping addiction.

She is retired and living on her own in a small terraced house with a lovely garden. Her treasured music room houses her piano, instruments and sheet music, along with encroaching paperwork. Her very cluttered sitting room had thousands of CDs, cassettes and record albums on every conceivable surface along with the many photographs and souvenirs of her trips to hear and participate in music festivals both here and abroad. It also contained many furnishings that she had inherited from her family that she no longer wanted to keep.

Below: Our contributor was determined to reclaim her guest room from the mountains of unwanted shopping that she had accrued (left). After a tough clear out, we were able to create a pretty space for visitors in the future (right).

Before

After

How it feels to let things go

The most troublesome areas were the two upstairs bedrooms, long since unrecognizable with the overwhelming number of charity shop purchases. Hundreds of bin-liners stacked floor to ceiling in the uninhabitable guest room were a constant reminder of her shopping habits. Realizing she needed help, she sought professional help with her shopping problems, but her physical health problems prevented her from tackling the job of clearing her space on her own. She asked for our help to turn her home back into a more organized space where she would be able to relax and entertain friends.

The goals
- Go through each and every bin-liner and determine what would stay, what would be donated to charity, recycled, sold or destroyed.
- Create a comfortable guest room to provide lodging for musical events.
- Organize and edit the music collection to be more accessible.
- Deal with family possessions.
- Look at past purchases to see problem areas and develop strategies to keep things in check.
- Reclaim the bedroom as a peaceful and relaxing space.

Below: No room in our contributor's house was free from unwanted clothes and unopened shopping bags – not even her own bedroom (left). The *Life Laundry* team were able to change this into a truly restful space (right).

Before

After

Solutions

- **Coming to grips with your past can help you move on in the future.** By emptying the contents of each bin-liner and dividing all of her possessions by categories, it was easy for her to see how she kept purchasing the same items over and over again. Looking at how many items still had price tags affixed showed that it was the purchasing rather than the using that had become the routine.

- **You can't erase the past.** Our contributor felt it was time to let go of all objects from her childhood that she did not associate with happy times. She wished to pass some of them on to her cousin and sell the rest to antique shops or at a car boot sale. Going to extremes and getting rid of everything at one time may not be the best approach. We were pleased to be able to refurbish and adapt many old items to a happy new life and use.

- **Swept away by the moment** – souvenirs and mementoes if collected over time can really add up. It's understandable to want to capture pleasant memories but, when space is at a premium, think about where the object can fit comfortably in your home. After years spent participating in folk festivals, our contributor amassed bin-liners filled with paraphernalia commemorating all of her outings. Stuck away in the junk room, they were never used or looked at, so many of them were consigned to the crusher to make way for a new phase of her life.

- **Control your passions.** Not allowed music as a child, this was a particularly difficult area to keep in check, and one that the contributor was firm in wanting to keep. My suggestions of editing some of the titles that perhaps were not listened to were met with determined resistance. She managed to reduce the quantity a bit, but not significantly. With no previous order or structure to how the music was stored, it was unlikely that even a tenth of the collection was played. By building shelves to contain over a thousand CDs then putting them in alphabetical order, she could then be able to better control her collection.

- **Getting rid of things you never use can give you back your space.** A whopping 171 bin-liners filled with clothing and craft material were sent off to the local charity. By clearing the spare bedroom, the makeover team were able to turn it into a warm and inviting space. Getting rid of all the charity shop clothing stored in her bedroom transformed the space into a relaxing place to sleep.

The outcome

A great success story: she has gone on to clear and redecorate many additional rooms, including the kitchen and bathroom, and every week she takes books to the local charity shop. She is now comfortable inviting people into her home, and she is better able to play and enjoy her music.

Taking responsibility for yourself

There are many situations in life that bring us to a new stage in our growth. Divorce or bereavement are common times when we face changes in our responsibilities and, as they are always mixed with emotions, it can often be unsettling. If you have suffered a loss early in your life, either through divorce or death, you may have been required to take on additional responsibilities within your family at an early age. In some cases it may even set you apart from your contemporaries.

No matter what your age, any change in routine takes getting used to. Whether you are now living on your own after years with partners or children, or setting up your first household, moving forward and getting settled in the routine practice of addressing things that need to get done will help you adapt to your new lifestyle. Letting go of things that are no longer relevant to your new situation can help make more space and room for new people and things to enter your life.

One of the greatest lessons you can learn in life is to be at peace with yourself. Feeling good about how you live your life will help you to maximize your talents and enable to reach your highest potential. When you take pride in your home and your profession, you surely make the most effort to do your personal best.

Accepting your failures and your losses and moving on

Any behaviour or situation that makes you feel bad about yourself, for whatever reason, will keep you stuck exactly where you are. If you spend more time worrying and apologizing about how things are rather than taking any steps to change the situation, you are selling yourself short. You can master anything you spend your time and attention on, even if it is only by taking a very small step at a time.

When clutter gets out of control in your home, each day you are confronted with your failure to address the issues in your life. For many contributors, keeping up with the paperwork seems to be a big problem, and it often means they are not paying attention to their financial affairs. Another common problem is the inability to address items relating to past events. Often the items hold painful memories that are a constant reminder of the event that happened in the past. By learning to forgive and forget the events of the past, and letting go of the physical reminders, you can move forward in your life and encourage new beginnings.

Give yourself a break. One of the most important ways of developing self-esteem is to take action. Stop using the events of the past as an excuse for not getting on in the present. Learn from your failures and let them go, along with all the stuff associated with it.

CASE STUDY 5: LEAVING HOME

When you first leave home, your newfound independence can often result in ignoring the day-to-day responsibilities of living on your own. With no one to tell you what you have to do and when you have to it, it is easy to develop bad habits that, if left unchecked, can develop into safety and hygiene issues along with limiting your ability to socialize.

Our twenty-something single man left his mother's home two years ago to move into a small flat on his own. His work in the travel industry required him to be out of town for days in a row, leaving little time to stay on top of household affairs. To supplement his income, he did market research for various companies. This generated significant amounts of paperwork, leaving his tiny flat inundated in projects that needed completion.

His father had left home when he was younger, and he was looked after, in part, by his grandmother and great aunt, who were avid collectors of figurines. He started his first piggy bank collection at an early age and saved money at the same time. Over the years his keen eye and love of antiques helped him to amass a sizeable and valuable collection that was haphazardly displayed and stored in several rooms of his home. There were so many boxes stored in what should have been the bedroom that he had never been able to use it for that purpose. He slept in the sitting room with all the clutter.

Both his grandmother and great-aunt passed away during this time, and he had

Below: With so much clutter suffocating the sitting room, no wonder our contributor's china collections were frequently lost or damaged (left). De-junking unearthed pretty pieces of furniture around which to base the room's look (right).

Before

After

many unopened boxes of their belongings that he was unable to tackle. Rather than appreciating the items and their happy memories, he let them lie unceremoniously amid the suitcases, clothing and other items that accumulated throughout his home. He wanted to regain control of his space to enable him to work, entertain, relax and enjoy his lovely possessions.

Below: The contents of our contributor's wardrobe had got out of control and had taken over his entire bedroom, forcing him to sleep in the sitting room (left). Re-claiming the bedroom and organizing the wardrobe properly was a priority (right).

The goals

- Come to terms with the mountains of unopened paperwork that made it impossible to get around the flat safely, and put in place a system to be able to stay on top of it.
- Create a work area to help stay organized.
- Reclaim the bedroom for a space to sleep and store clothing, and for travel-related items.
- Protect and look after valuable items properly.
- Create a sitting room and dining room to be able to have social functions.
- Confront items that have emotional meaning and decide which to keep, sell, give away or junk.
- Develop storage solutions to make the most of small-space living.

Before

After

Solutions

- **Before you can get on with the present, you must confront the past.** Accumulated and unopened paperwork make it impossible to stay on top of your current affairs. Over the weekend we were able to get rid of years' worth of unnecessary paperwork, making it easier to set up current files for the work at hand.
- **Sleep is an important way to recharge our energy.** Our contributor was constantly surrounded by vast quantities of clutter and had to clear the bed each night before going to sleep. One of our first priorities was to reclaim the bedroom for sleeping and storing his clothing and personal items.
- **Separate work and pleasure.** It is difficult to entertain or relax when you have mounds of unfinished work surrounding you. By setting aside a small area in the corner of his sitting room for a built-in work area, the remainder of the large room could be used for dining and relaxation, keeping the two activities separated.
- **Don't live out of a suitcase.** Make wherever you are your home. The first thing I do whenever I travel is to unpack my suitcase. When away, it makes me feel like I'm in a home away from home. When I return, it makes it easier to get back into my normal routine.
- **Show off your prized possessions.** Find the best means of displaying your objects. Using many of the lovely furnishings our contributor acquired over the years, we were able to show off his treasured collections. The most precious were stored in glass-fronted cabinets, others on the mantelpiece and built-in shelving units.
- **Transform your space.** In one of the most transformational makeovers of the series, a cluttered and littered sitting, dining, sleeping and workroom was transformed into a mini-Versailles Palace reception room using furnishings that were hidden under years' worth of clutter. By getting rid of rubbish you can find at least 30 per cent more space in each room.
- **Revisit emotional possessions.** We go through many stages in the bereavement process and we all do it in our own time. If you are unable to tackle these items in the early stages of the loss, don't let them sit there forever. Look for the treasured moments and reminders to keep and let go of any that cause you pain.
- **Small spaces require clever storage solutions.** In a tiny flat, even the smallest area needs to be used to its greatest advantage. High-level shelving in the entranceway provided suitable storage for books, photos and precious possessions and became an attractive design feature.

The outcome

Accepting responsibility for himself for the first time, our contributor has managed to stay up to date with the paperwork and keep his home clutter-free. A weekly cleaner helps him stay on top of the chores. The experience of going through his deceased relatives' possessions has allowed him to come to terms with their death.

Life after *The Life Laundry*

I would like to give a big thank you to all of our amazing contributors who participated in *The Life Laundry* series. They have opened up their homes, and their lives, to help themselves – and in the process many others – to see how possessions can prevent you from making the most of your living space and accomplishing what you want in your life.

In many cases, the process is an emotional one. Years' worth of unfinished business is brought to the surface to be addressed, once and for all. Seeing is believing, as the saying goes, and the initial shock of our contributors as they faced up to their hoarding habits, when their possessions are gathered together for the first time on the lawn, is all that is needed to get the process under way. With the support of family or friends, our contributors begin the process of shedding years' worth of unwanted stuff and unwanted emotions to give them back a part of their home.

We don't do the hard work – they do. We simply facilitate the process and provide the reward. How much they learn from the process and carry on streamlining their home depends on them.

When we begin the de-cluttering process on the lawn, we often start with the least emotional items to help our contributors get into the swing of letting things go. Not everything we hold on to has sentimental or emotional attachment. Some things just accumulate out of bad habits and a lack of organization.

Things like newspapers, magazines and household paperwork are always a good place to begin. You may not like having to do it, but it isn't going to make you cry! Tackle these areas first to feel the immediate lightness of being at having accomplished a task that had been put off for too long.

Clutter can often lead to problems with self-esteem, as your inability to keep on top of things is something that you face every day. Each area that you are able to tackle and reduce will make you feel more positive about yourself.

Looking after the things that you own is the way you show appreciation on a daily basis for all that you have. When you appreciate what you own, you are living in the present moment. You look at or use all of the things you have around you and you feel at home in your space. Appreciation is a feeling that comes from the heart. When you are thankful, you accept that you have what you need to be happy in that moment. The moment you make that leap of acceptance, you will find that you truly need very little to be happy.

Stockists

General household suppliers

Debenhams
Furniture, bedlinen, window dressings and lighting.
Tel: 020 7408 4444
www.debenhams.com

Habitat
Contemporary furniture, bedlinen, lighting and storage accessories.
Tel: 0845 601 0740
www.habitat.co.uk

Heal's
Contemporary furniture, fabrics, lighting and accessories.
Tel: 020 7636 1666
www.heals.co.uk

Ikea
Affordable flatpack furniture; wall-mounted fittings; furnishings, fabrics and lighting.
Tel: 020 8208 5600
www.ikea.co.uk

John Lewis
Wide range of furniture, fabrics, wallpapers, window dressings, lighting and accessories.
Tel: 020 7629 7711
www.johnlewis.co.uk

Marks & Spencer
Range of furniture, wall-mounted fittings; towel and bath sets; curtains, bedlinen and lighting.
Tel: 020 7935 4422 for stockists,
0845 603 1603 for mail order
www.marksandspencer.com

Next Home
Furniture, wallpaper, paints, curtains, blinds and lighting; bed and bath accessories.
Tel: 0870 243 5435 for stockists,
0845 600 7000 for mail order
www.next.co.uk

Kitchens

Alno UK
Innovative designs featuring the latest colours and materials.
Tel: 020 8898 4781
www.alno.co.uk

Crown Imperial
High-quality fitted kitchens in a range of styles and finishes.
Tel: 01227 742424
www.crown-imperial.co.uk

MFI Homeworks
Wide range of affordable styles.
Tel: 0870 241 0154
www.mfi.co.uk

Nolte
Huge choice of contemporary designs, including pale wood, coloured and frosted glass units.
Tel: 01279 868800
www.nolte-kuechen.de

Paula Rosa
Quality kitchens in many styles.
Tel: 01903 746666
www.paularosa.com

Plain & Simple Kitchens
Designs ranging from handpainted wood to sleek stainless steel door fronts.
Tel: 0161 839 8983
www.plainandsimplekitchens.com

Poggenpohl
Cutting-edge contemporary designs in woods and laminates.
Tel: 01604 763482
www.poggenpohl.de

Bathrooms

Armitage Shanks
Suites for every setting, from cottage-style to contemporary.
Tel: 0800 866 966
www.armitage-shanks.co.uk

Bathroom Discount Centre
Discounts on famous-name bathroom fittings.
Tel: 020 7381 4222
www.bathroomdiscount.co.uk

Colourwash
Contemporary designer-style fittings, including coloured glass and stainless steel basins.
Tel: 020 8947 5578
www.colourwash.co.uk

Dolphin Bathrooms
Styles ranging from country cottage to city chic, some including furniture, with complete design and installation service.
Tel: 0800 626717
www.dolphinbathrooms.com

Ideal-Standard
Wide range of contemporary and classic fittings, including suites designed to fit into small spaces.
Tel: 01482 346461
www.ideal-standard.co.uk

The Imperial Bathroom Co
Traditional-style suites and storage furniture.
Tel: 01922 743074
www.imperial-bathrooms.co.uk

Magnet
Modern and traditional suites, including roll-top and whirlpool baths; computer-aided planning.
Branches nationwide.
www.magnet.co.uk

Twyford Bathrooms
Wide range of modern, classic and Art Deco suites and taps at prices to suit every pocket.
Tel: 0870 840 1000
www.twyfordbathrooms.com

Flooring

Allied Carpets
Carpet superstores with a huge range of colours and patterns.
Tel: 01689 895000
www.alliedcarpets.com

Crucial Trading
Natural floorcoverings and rugs in sisal, coir and seagrass.
Tel: 01562 743747
www.crucial-trading.com

Dalsouple
Rubber flooring in many colours.
Tel: 01278 727777
www.dalsouple.com

Fired Earth
Marble, slate and terracotta tiles.
Tel: 01295 814300
www.firedearth.com

Window treatments

The Curtain Exchange
Quality secondhand curtains bought and sold.
Tel: 020 7731 8316
www.thecurtainexchange.cwc.net

Luxaflex
Made-to-measure blinds in modern styles, including Venetian and pinoleum.
Tel: 08000 399399
www.luxaflex.com

Prêt à Vivre
Curtains and blinds made to measure; poles and tiebacks.
Tel: 0845 130 5161
www.pretavivre.com

Rosebys
Ready-made curtains and blinds.
Tel: 0800 052 0493
www.rosebys.com

Furniture and storage

Andrew Macintosh Furniture
Handpainted designs in Bauhaus, Shaker and English country styles.
Tel: 020 8995 8333
www.andrewmacintoshfurniture.co.uk

Cargo Home Shop
Dining furniture, affordable cookware and tableware. Sofas upholstered to order.
Tel: 01844 261800

The Conran Shop
Contemporary designer furniture.
Tel: 020 7589 7401
www.conran.co.uk

The Cotswold Company
Storage furniture and baskets in wood and woven fibres.
Tel: 0870 550 2233
www.cotswoldco.com

Cucina Direct
Cookware, gadgets, storage aids and small appliances.
Tel: 020 8246 4311
www.cucinadirect.co.uk

The Dormy house
Blanket boxes and bedside tables sold ready to paint; headboards upholstered to order.
Tel: 01264 365789
www.thedormyhouse.com

Ducal
Solid wood furniture in traditional designs, including four posters.
Tel: 01264 333666
www.ducal-furniture.co.uk

Ercol
Solid wood furniture including wood-framed sofas.
Tel: 01844 271800
www.ercol.com

The Holding Company
Contemporary storage furniture and accessories.
Tel: 020 8445 2888
www.theholdingcompany.co.uk

Lakeland Limited
Storage fittings for organizing wardrobe and drawer space.
Tel: 015394 88100
www.lakelandlimited.co.uk

The Pier
Ethnic-style furniture ranges in dark wood, bamboo and rattan.
Tel: 0845 609 1234
www.pier.co.uk

Purves & Purves
Innovative designer furniture, including Italian sofas.
Tel: 020 7580 8223 for stockists; 020 8993 2064 for mail order
www.purves.co.uk

Rhode Design
Handmade furniture; high-tech and Shaker-style MDF units that can be painted to order.
Tel: 020 7354 9933

Scotts of Stow
Tableware, cookware and farmhouse-style furniture.
Tel: 0870 600 4444 www.scottsofstow.co.uk

Scumble Goosie
Ready-to-paint furniture in classic designs.
Tel: 01453 731305
www.scumblegoosie.com

Shaker
Shaker-style wooden furniture, peg rails and oval storage boxes.
Tel: 020 7935 9461
www.shaker.co.uk

Sharps bedrooms
Fully fitted storage systems made to measure.
Tel: 0800 917 8178

Wickes
Affordable fitted furniture ready for DIY assembly.
Tel: 0870 608 9001
www.wickes.co.uk

Paints, wallpapers and fabrics

Anna French
Floral and paint-effect wallpapers; printed cotton fabrics, lace and sheers.
Tel: 020 7349 1099

Cath Kidston
Retro 1950s-style floral cottons.
Tel: 020 7221 4000 for stockists,
020 7229 8000 for mail order
www.cathkidston.co.uk

Colefax & Fowler
Florals on linen and chintz, and complementary wallpapers.
Tel: 020 8877 6400

Coloroll
Contemporary wallcoverings and coordinating bedlinen.
Tel: 0800 056 4878 (bedlinen), 0161 351 3000 (wallcoverings)
www.coloroll.co.uk

Crown Paints
Vast choice of shades, including the Kitchen & Bathroom range and the extensive mix-to-order Expressions collection.
Tel: 01254 704951
www.crownpaint.co.uk]

Designers Guild
Colourful contemporary fabrics, wallpapers, paints and bedlinen.
Tel: 020 7351 5775
www.designersguild.com

Dulux
Vast choice of colours, including the Kitchens & Bathrooms range and the extensive mix-to-order Colour Mixing System.
Tel: 01753 550555
www.dulux.co.uk

Farrow & Ball
Heritage paint shades.
Tel: 01202 876141
www.farrow-ball.co.uk

Osborne & Little
Classic and contemporary prints, weaves and wallpapers.
Tel: 020 7352 1456
www.osborneandlittle.com

Sanderson
Extensive paint, fabric and wallpaper collections with coordinated bedlinen ranges.
Tel: 01895 830000
www.sanderson uk.com

Lighting

Christopher Wray Lighting
Huge range of light fittings, from traditional to cutting-edge.
Tel: 020 7736 8434   www.christopher-wray.com

John Cullen Lighting
Discreet modern lighting, such as spots and downlighters.
Tel: 020 7371 5400   www.johncullenlighting.co.uk

McCloud & co
Vast choice of light fittings by British craftspeople, available in a selection of different finishes.
Tel: 020 7352 1533
www.mccloud.co.uk

Ryness
Well-made light fittings, including recessed eyeball ceiling lights.
Tel: 020 7278 8993
www.ryness.co.uk

SKK lights
Innovative light fittings, including some wacky designs.
Tel: 020 7434 4095
www.skk.net

The Stiffkey Lampshop
Original and reproduction lamps, candlesticks and candelabra.
Tel: 01328 830460

Wax Lyrical
Decorative candles and candleholders.
Tel: 020 8561 0235
www.waxlyrical.co.uk

Further reading

Organization/de-cluttering

Calm at Work
Paul Wilson
Penguin Books, 1998

Clear your Clutter with Feng Shui
Karen Kingston
Piatkus, 1998

Go for it!
Dawna Walter
Quadrille Publishing Ltd, 2003

The Life Laundry: How to De-Junk Your Life
Dawna Walter, Mark Franks
BBC Worldwide, 2002

New Leaf, New Life
Dawna Walter
Quadrille Publishing Ltd, 2001

Organized Living
Dawna Walter with Helen Chislett
Conran Octopus, 1999

Homes/Interiors

The Feng Shui House Book
Gina Lazenby
Conran Octopus, 2003

Paint Effects Manual
Kerry Skinner
Apple Press, 2003

Spaces for Living
Liz Bauwens and Alexandra Campbell
Collins and Brown, 1999

Healing methods

Essential Reiki
Diane Stein
Crossing Press, 1995

The Healing Handbook
Tara Ward
Arcturus, 2000

Miracles of Mind
Russell Targ, Jane Katra Ph.D.
New World Library, 1998

Spiritual Development

Anatomy of the Spirit
Caroline Myss, Ph.D
Bantam, 1997

The Power of Now
Eckhart Tolle
Hodder and Stoughton, 2001

A Harmony of Angels
Angela McGerr
Quadrille Publishing Ltd, 2001

The Artist's Way
Julia Cameron
Souvenir Press, 1995

For further development

Helplines

Bereavement
Cruse Bereavement Line
National line: 0870 167 1677
www.crusebereavementcare.org.uk

Daily Motivation
Thought for Today
www.innerspace.org.uk/home/
thoughtfortoday.asp

Emotional Support
Samaritans
0845 790 9090
www.samaritans.co.uk

Free Courses on Self Development
www.brahmakumaris.org.uk

Meditation
Transcendental Meditation
www.transcendental-meditation.org.uk

Recycling
Waste Watch Wasteline
0870 243 0136

On the Internet:
www.wasteonline.org.uk

Textile Recycling for Aid and International
Development
020 8733 2580

Stress Management
International Stress Management
Organization
07000 780430
www.isma.org.uk

Yoga
British Wheel of Yoga
01529 306851
www.bwy.org.uk

Charities

To find a local charity, check Yellow Pages
listings

On the Internet:
www.charitychoice.co.uk

Car boot sales

Car Boot & Fairs Calendar
www.carbootcalendar.com

Index

Acknowledgements

Thanks to:

Nicky Ross, Rachel Copus, Julia Zimmermann, Sarah Ponder and Robin Wood of BBC Worldwide and all at Grade Design for being such great *Life Laundry* fans and producing books to be proud of.

Andy Stockley for taking the time to do up the plans and photos and everyone at APE Designs – Phil, Lucy, Max, Paul, Tony and anyone I've left out, for the makeover magic.

Daisy Goodwin, Jerry Foulkes, Sara Woodford, Cat Ledger at Talkback who have continued to shape the vision of the programme and the book. Carrie Britten and Susie Worster for work on the past series. Vics, Steve and Jude, *Life Laundry* office-based staff who have looked after the production.

A special thank you to Jo Clinton-Davis, Executive Producer for the BBC, for caring so much about the project.

The *Life Laundry* team – an awesome force to enter into our contributors' lives. Made up of presenters, directors, researchers, makeover team, runners and security, 20 people take over our contributors' homes and lives for five days. During this brief period of time, each and every team member works non-stop towards the common goal of getting through the clutter to help make the experience a life-changing moment.

All of the directors from series two and three – Stephen, Simon, Anna, Susannah, James, Martyn and Tina for crafting beautiful programmes to watch. To a girl's best friend – the camera men – the lovely Graham, Martin and Chris who always manage to be at the right place at the right time, and all the soundmen for never letting a plane get in the way of a good moment.

The brilliant researchers who make the stories happen – Lizzy and Lizzie, James, Sam, Kirsty and Harry and the unflappable location manager, Jane, for co-ordinating the impossible.

All the runners and assistants who shoulder much of the hard work – Rob, Sam, Sacha, Paula, and Andrew.

The following for their contributions to the programme: ABC Spax, Addis & Bal, Akzo Nobel Decorative Coatings Ltd, Bedeck, Betterware, Campaign Marketing PR, Click Systems Ltd, Crown, Curver Rubbermaid, Dorma, Earlex Ltd , Electrolux, Farrow & Ball, Fired Earth, Habitat, Henkel, ICI Paints, ITW Construction Products, Jackie Biggin Media, Makita, Mason Williams PR, Matalan, McCann Erickson, Muji, Paslode, Plasplugs Ltd, Polycell, Price's Candles, Riverdale Flooring, Romerco, Rowenta, Screwfix Direct Ltd, Spreckley, Stanley, Town & Country, Wallace HCL.

Special thanks to Caroline, who always inspires me to look my best.

Bella Whitely, for the design inspiration and helping our contributors' dreams come true. Mark Franks, for always passing on such good information and providing a good laugh in series one and two.

Last, but not least, Tex and Rob, who never find anything too difficult to accomplish and are always there to help with everything. Cheers!